SCOTTISH MYSTERIES

Donald M Fraser

MERCAT PRESS
EDINBURGH

First published in 1997 by Mercat Press
James Thin, 53 South Bridge, Edinburgh EH1 1YS

© Donald M Fraser, 1997

ISBN 1873644 752

Set in Plantin at Mercat Press
Printed and bound in Great Britain by
Athenæum Press Ltd, Gateshead, Tyne & Wear

This is for Hollie Kiera—and me

CONTENTS

ILLUSTRATIONS

ACKNOWLEDGEMENTS

In attempting to produce a book of this kind, it is necessary to carry out painstaking and thorough research into each mystery. To do this can take many months, and sometimes years, to complete. I would have been foolish to ever think that I could do all of this alone.

In the course of my research, I approached many individuals and not one refused to help. They, like me, became intrigued by the mysteries and determined to unearth the facts in an effort to reveal the truth. The time to thank them has arrived.

As usual, I am indebted to my friend (I nearly wrote 'old friend') and fellow author Jim Barr in far off Nutfield, Victoria, Australia, for his constant encouragement and help in tracking down information relating to the principals in Chapter 2. If I set him a task that he couldn't help with, he always knew someone who could. One of those he enlisted to the cause was Paul Roser of the Old Jail Museum in Melbourne, Australia, who provided me with valuable assistance and information on the life and times of Ned Kelly, and for which he is due my profound thanks.

David Fowler, Senior Librarian at the Stornoway Public Library, Isle of Lewis responded to more of my pleas for help. As on a previous occasion, he provided me with a wealth of material, this time on the Flannen Isles (Chapter 5), so much so, I felt I could have written an entire book on the mystery. I am, once again, deeply indebted to him.

David Howitt, Isle of Mull, is another who needs to be acknowledged and thanked. He is one of those people who unselfishly shared his information and thoughts with me. As can be seen from the text in Chapter 10, Mr Howitt features personally in this mystery and has written his own book on the subject. It is also the case that I believe he pointed me in the right direction when I was having difficulty in trying to unravel the complicated details of events. Thanks are also due to him for allowing the use of photographs from his book.

Thanks to Neil Owen of Oban for his expertise in matters aeronautical in relation to Chapter 8. I must also add that when this chapter was at the planning stage, he was responsible for opening my eyes to certain facts, hitherto unknown to me.

My gratitude also to author Euan Macpherson of Dundee for sharing with me his information on the life of William Henry Bury (Chapter 3). His help was much appreciated.

In more general terms, my thanks go to Ian Bell, a colleague of mine who has recently developed a dread of dogs, and his long-suffering wife Jean, for being unofficial readers of the manuscript, correcting mistakes, suggesting alternatives and being blunt about it all.

My thanks to Helen and Tracy for the patience they showed in going along with my many requests to copy this and to copy that. They always smiled.

Last but not least, my belated thanks to Gus Britton of the Royal Navy Submarine Museum in Gosport in Hampshire. Sadly, Gus died before the completion of this book, but not before he passed on volumes of his knowledge of all things submarine to me. I am forever indebted to him.

BIOGRAPHY

Donald Fraser was born and brought up in Glasgow and still lives in the city with his wife and two children. He finished his education in the same year that comprehensive schools were brought in.

His writing is done mostly in the wee small hours, combining it, as he does, with a full-time job. Between both, his involvement with mysteries of one sort or another is continuous.

This is his second book and he is currently working on numerous ideas for his third.

FOREWORD

It has been said that for everything that occurs there is an answer and that the answer will be known only when the truth is told. If that were the case, then there would be no mysteries in our lives.

The expression 'the truth is out there' is a popular saying today and I make no excuse for quoting it now, except to suggest that what it is saying is, in itself, true. The truth *is* out there—at the bottom of our seas, on the tops of our mountains or even on some dusty shelf in a public or private archive. The problem seems to be one of not knowing where to look for the facts, and on occasions when we do find the right place, the mystery is complicated further by the complete truth not being provided.

For a great many years I have been fascinated by certain types of mysteries. I tried to read everything that I could about them, believing that the books I read gave me all the facts about the various events. What surprised me most when I came to research the material for this book was that I had never once, while reading those books, been in receipt of all the facts.

To me, there appeared to be two main reasons for this 'misinformation'. One reason is the author's sloppy and incomplete research of the subject. The second, and I suspect this to be the more important, was that certain facts did not fit in with the author's conclusions on the mystery and therefore, these 'extra' facts were conveniently omitted. As I have no wish to be accused of doing the same thing, I have related in the text all the facts that I have discovered. When I have felt competent to do so, I have also made comments about them.

While I make no claims to have solved, beyond doubt, any of the mysteries in this book, I have tried to include in each chapter what I believe to be reasoned and sensible conclusions or suggestions. Should the reader wish to draw his or her own conclusions, then so much the better.

The ten mysteries featured in this book are only a small selection of the many that pepper Scotland's history.

One
THE KILLER DOCTOR

The mystery starts about twelve years ago but the story begins over 130 years ago.

At the bottom end of the Saltmarket in Glasgow, next to the River Clyde, sits a squat, but nonetheless impressive, sandstone building. Completed in 1812, it is known to all as the city's High Court of Justiciary.

In the nineteenth century, with capital punishment still on the statute books, Glasgow witnessed a great many public executions, which were carried out opposite the Courthouse at the entrance to Glasgow Green, the city's most famous public park. This location became known as Jail Square and between the years 1814 and 1865, it was the scene of 52 hangings—an average of one a year!

The building housed not only a Court but an official prison too, where all those condemned to death would spend the time between being sentenced and the punishment being carried out in the cells below. As a consequence of this, a tunnel was constructed leading from the Courthouse below the busy Saltmarket and emerging beside the scaffold, which was erected specially for each occasion.

In 1985, the Courthouse underwent a renovation programme. Included in the work was the tunnel, as it had been unused for 120 years and had fallen into a state of disrepair. Fears were expressed that the roadway above it, with its huge volume of modern day traffic, could cause it to cave in. The decision was taken to fill in the underground passageway.

About nine or ten feet into the tunnel, from the Courthouse side, one of the workmen discovered a secret hiding place in one of the walls. The niche held a pair of brown leather boots, still in good

1

'Dr' Edward Pritchard

condition. Closer examination revealed that in one of the boots was a neatly folded piece of what appeared to be greaseproof or tissue paper.

As the workman gently unfolded the paper, it disintegrated in his hands as it had completely dried out. Beyond the paper however, he found he was now holding a quantity of human hair.

The shaken workman brought his find to the attention of his supervisors, who in turn inspected the items. The boots were of a button-fastening type, a style that was in fashion in the nineteenth century. The hair was black in colour. As the tunnel had been deserted all those years ago and the hiding place well concealed, two questions arose: who had been the owner of both the boots and hair, and who had hidden them?

No one at the time, or since, has come up with an answer to these puzzles, perhaps because the finds date from so long ago. Maybe that is the case, but what follows on the next few pages is what could be the answer to these intriguing mysteries.

The story starts six years before the last recorded use of the tunnel, when in 1859, a Dr Edward William Pritchard, his wife, Mary Jane, and their children came to live in Glasgow. The family moved to the city from Yorkshire, primarily because the doctor had got himself into some trouble there.

His problems stemmed from the fact that he was an incorrigible liar, arrogant and something of a ladies' man. These faults had combined to reduce his public standing so much that his patients had lost confidence in him and his medical practice suffered as a result. He sold up and decided to start afresh.

Unfortunately for Pritchard, his reputation in medical circles followed him to Glasgow. He could find no other doctor in the city willing to propose him for membership as a Fellow of the Faculty of Physicians and Surgeons. Undaunted, he then applied for the vacant Andersonian Chair of Surgery at Glasgow University and provided forged references in support of his application! He was soon found out.

In 1863, the Pritchards were resident in Berkeley Terrace, when a fire broke out in the room of a servant girl. She was killed, apparently due to asphyxiation, but suspicions surrounded her death. Although the fire started in her room, subsequent investigations showed that she had made no attempt to escape the blaze. The conclusion was drawn that she was either unconscious or dead before the fire began.

Rumours were rife that Pritchard and the servant girl were lovers and that she had become pregnant by him but refused to have an abortion. The girl had then decided to break her silence on the matter by telling Mrs Pritchard, which basically sealed her fate. However, there was never enough evidence and no one was ever charged over the matter.

A year later, the Pritchards moved to a bigger house at 131 Sauchiehall Street, Glasgow. The house was large enough to accommodate the family and servants and also Pritchard's consulting rooms. It was in these rooms that Mrs Pritchard discovered her husband in a tender embrace with a 15-year-old servant girl, Mary MacLeod, of whom we shall learn more later.

Within weeks of this incident, at the start of November 1864, Mrs Pritchard became ill and took to her bed. Throughout the month, she gradually improved, until she was well enough to go and stay with her mother in Edinburgh in an effort to recuperate fully.

Mary Jane Pritchard (left) and Mrs Taylor, both victims of the killer doctor

With her health restored, she returned to Glasgow in time for the Christmas celebrations that year. In her absence, her husband had, on 8th December, purchased from a chemist in Sauchiehall Street, one ounce of a mixture called Flemming's Tincture of Aconite, which was six times stronger than the ordinary tincture, along with quantities of antimony, which is another poison, and chloroform. Pritchard was to make three similar purchases in as many months.

Within days of her return, Mrs Pritchard fell ill again with the same symptoms as before. Again, she took to her bed, and remained there until she died, three months later. All through January 1865, Mrs Pritchard's illness got progressively worse until, on 1st February, she was in unbearable pain. Pritchard called in a Dr Cowan from Edinburgh, who was also a distant relative of Mrs Pritchard. However, Cowan did not consider her to be seriously ill.

That same night, with no improvement in her condition, Pritchard sent for another doctor, a Dr Gairdner. This doctor treated her that night and again on a second visit a day or so later, but Pritchard decided, for whatever reasons, that Gairdner was not to call again.

Gairdner, his suspicions aroused, wrote to Mrs Pritchard's brother, Michael Taylor, in Penrith, Cumbria, and who, coincidentally, was also a medical man. Gairdner recommended in his letter that Mrs Pritchard be removed from her home and when this was suggested by

4

her brother, Pritchard agreed but stated that she was too ill even to travel.

When news of these affairs reached the ears of Mrs Pritchard's mother in Edinburgh, she travelled through to Glasgow on the first available train. Pritchard was no doubt surprised to find his mother-in-law, Mrs Taylor, in attendance at his wife's bedside. But her concern for her daughter's health was to prove fatal.

Pritchard was now on the horns of a dilemma. He was, in fact, slowly poisoning his wife. There was no way he could continue to do this while her mother was present. Also, his mother-in-law, a few hours after her arrival, had caught him in a compromising position with Mary MacLeod in the consulting rooms. When discovered, Pritchard had hidden his mistress in a cupboard and flatly denied the allegations his mother-in-law made. What could he do?

He did not take long in deciding what course of action he should take. The day after she arrived, Mrs Taylor fell ill with the same symptoms that were plaguing her daughter after eating some tapioca from a packet. The callous doctor had decided to poison her too!

Mrs Taylor took to her daughter's room and remained there night and day. She recovered sufficiently to be able to minister to her daughter's every need until about 10 o'clock on the night of 24th February. The house was quiet and still when a piercing scream echoed from Mrs Pritchard's bedroom.

The servants rushed to assist and found Mrs Taylor slumped at the foot of her daughter's bed, having convulsions. Pritchard was summoned and sent for a local doctor, Dr James Paterson.

Paterson examined Mrs Taylor and his diagnosis was that she had taken some powerful drug. Probably because of the location of the sick woman, he also examined Mrs Pritchard and came to the conclusion that she was suffering from antimony poisoning.

When Paterson informed Pritchard of his findings in the case of Mrs Taylor, Pritchard stated that she was in the habit of 'taking a drop'. Fortunately for Pritchard, Mrs Taylor was fond of taking Battley's Sedative Solution, an opium-based medicine, and she had a bottle of the concoction in her pocket that night.

Paterson was of the opinion that she had overdosed on it and that he could do nothing more for her as she was dying. His prediction was correct. Mrs Taylor died later, during the night.

Dr Paterson was asked by either Pritchard or her son, Michael Taylor, to provide a death certificate for Mrs Taylor but no matter which requested it, Paterson refused. Instead, he wrote to the Glasgow

EXTRACT ENTRY OF DEATH, IN TERMS OF 17° & 18° VICTORIÆ, CAP. 80, §§ 56 & 58.

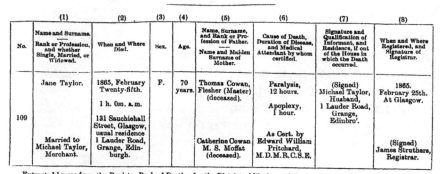

	(1)	(2)	(3)	(4)	(5)	(6)	(7)	(8)
No.	Name and Surname. Rank or Profession, and whether Single, Married, or Widowed.	When and Where Died.	Sex.	Age.	Name, Surname, and Rank or Profession of Father. — Name and Maiden Surname of Mother.	Cause of Death, Duration of Disease, and Medical Attendant by whom certified.	Signature and Qualification of Informant, and Residence, if out of the House in which the Death occurred.	When and Where Registered, and Signature of Registrar.
109	Jane Taylor.	1865, February Twenty-fifth. 1 h. 0m. a.m. 131 Sauchiehall Street, Glasgow, usual residence 1 Lauder Road, Grange, Edinburgh.	F.	70 years.	Thomas Cowan, Flesher (Master) (deceased).	Paralysis, 12 hours. Apoplexy, 1 hour.	(Signed) Michael Taylor, Husband, 1 Lauder Road, Grange, Edinbro'.	1865. February 25th. At Glasgow.
	Married to Michael Taylor, Merchant.				Catherine Cowan M. S. Moffat (deceased).	As Cert. by Edward William Pritchard, M.D.M.R.C.S.E.		(Signed) James Struthers, Registrar.

Extracted by me from the Register Book of Deaths, for the District of Blythswood, in the Burgh of Glasgow, this Seventh day of April, 1865. } JAMES STRUTHERS, *Registrar.*

Death certificate of Mrs Taylor provided by 'Dr' Pritchard

Registrar of Deaths, describing Mrs Taylor's death as 'sudden, unexpected and to me, mysterious'.

The Registrar, somewhat strangely, took no action upon receipt of the letter, other than to inform Pritchard that a death certificate was not being issued. Pritchard wasted no time in issuing a certificate signed by himself, citing the primary cause of death as paralysis and the secondary cause as apoplexy.

This was probably Pritchard's first major mistake. If apoplexy (loss of consciousness) occurs, then paralysis can follow, normally as the result of a burst blood vessel in the brain, but not the other way around.

Undaunted, Pritchard asked Dr Paterson to continue to attend his wife, which the doctor did, calling on her while Pritchard was in Edinburgh attending his mother-in-law's funeral at Grange Cemetery. Paterson's diagnosis was the same as before—Mrs Pritchard was suffering from the effects of antimony poisoning.

Matters remained steady for about two weeks until, on 13th March, Pritchard purchased his final ounce of aconite tincture, antimony and chloroform from the chemist. The same night, he sent his wife up some food for her supper, but Mrs Pritchard only took a small piece of the cheese and ordered it to be taken away as she didn't like the taste of it.

The maid was returning the cheese to the kitchen and took a piece for herself. She later gave a statement saying that the cheese had burned the back of her throat. The cook, who also couldn't resist taking a piece, became ill too.

Two days later, Mrs Pritchard drank a glass of an egg and sugar

EXTRACT ENTRY OF DEATH, IN TERMS OF 17° & 18° VICTORIÆ, CAP. 80, §§ 56 & 58.

	(1)	(2)	(3)	(4)	(5)	(6)	(7)	(8)
No.	Name and Surname. Rank or Profession, and whether Single, Married, or Widowed.	When and Where Died.	Sex.	Age.	Name, Surname, and Rank or Profession of Father. Name and Maiden Surname of Mother.	Cause of Death, Duration of Disease, and Medical Attendant by whom certified.	Signature and Qualification of Informant, and Residence, if out of the House in which the Death occurred.	When and Where Registered, and Signature of Registrar.
156	Mary Jane Pritchard. Married to Edward William Pritchard, M.D.	1865, March Eighteenth. 1 h. 0 m. a.m. 131 Sauchiehall Street, Glasgow.	F.	39 years.	Michael Taylor, Merchant. Jane Taylor M. S. Cowan (deceased).	Gastric Fever. Two Months. As Cert. by Edward William Pritchard, M.D.M.R.C.S.E.	(Signed) Edward William Pritchard. Husband. Present.	1865. March 20th. At Glasgow. (Signed) Gavin Buchanan, Assistant Registrar. (Initialed) J.S.

Extracted by me from the Register Book of Deaths, for the District of Blythswood, in the Burgh of Glasgow, this Seventh day of April, 1865. } JAMES STRUTHERS, Registrar.

Death certificate of Mary Jane Pritchard, again provided by 'Dr' Pritchard

mixture prepared by her husband and immediately became uncontrollably sick accompanied by severe pains. Again, the cook had also taken some of this mixture and she too had the same symptoms as her mistress.

Two days later again, on 17th March, in the early afternoon, Pritchard was seen giving his wife a drink, of what is not known, but almost as soon as she had swallowed it, she became violently ill which resulted in her becoming totally delirious.

Dr Paterson was called again and he wrote out a prescription for something to make Mrs Pritchard sleep. Later that night, Mrs Pritchard finally died. Allegedly distraught, Pritchard still had enough presence of mind to ask Paterson for a death certificate for his wife. Once again, Paterson refused.

Pritchard completed the death certificate himself, citing gastric fever as the cause. He then began immediate preparations to have his wife's body interred beside that of her mother in Edinburgh.

Two days after Mrs Pritchard's death, on 20th March, Glasgow's Procurator Fiscal, Mr Gemmell, opened his mail and found a letter suggesting that he should investigate the two deaths. The letter was signed by someone using a pseudonym, but it is almost an accepted fact that the author was none other than Dr James Paterson, although he strongly denied it.

Paterson, having seen his letter to the Registrar detailing his suspicions in the case of Mrs Taylor go without investigation, followed swiftly by the death of Mrs Pritchard, and believing her to also have been the victim of poison, must have found it extremely difficult to keep silent.

However, there can be no doubt that Paterson was in great turmoil

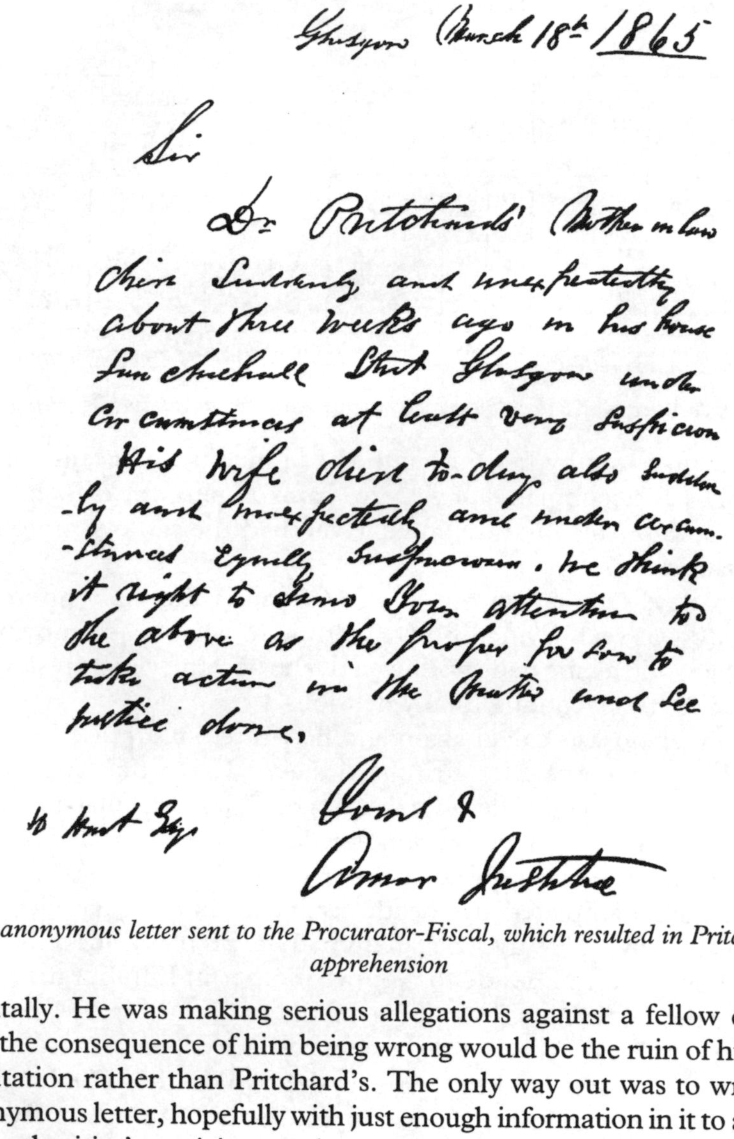

[handwritten letter]

Glasgow March 18th 1865

Sir

Dr Pritchards' [mother-in-law] died suddenly and unexpectedly about three weeks ago in his house Sun Michall Street Glasgow under circumstances at least very suspicion His wife died to-day, also suddenly and unexpectedly and under circumstances equally suspicious. we think it right to draw your attention to the above as the proper person to take action in the matter and see justice done,

To Hart Esq.

Yours &

Amor Justitia

The anonymous letter sent to the Procurator-Fiscal, which resulted in Pritchard's apprehension

mentally. He was making serious allegations against a fellow doctor and the consequence of him being wrong would be the ruin of his own reputation rather than Pritchard's. The only way out was to write an anonymous letter, hopefully with just enough information in it to arouse the authorities' suspicions and start enquiries into both matters.

What Paterson did not know was that Pritchard had come to the notice of the Procurator Fiscal's department before, thanks to the 1863 house fire.

Gemmell immediately called on Superintendent McCall, the Officer-in-Charge of the Central Police District. Together, they called at the Registrar's Office in order to view both death certificates for themselves. While there, the Registrar commented on the letter written to him by Dr Paterson and the suspicions that he held. The existence of the letter had been unknown to Gemmell and McCall until this moment, but incredibly, this vital piece of evidence had been destroyed.

Immediately on leaving the Registrar's Office, they called on Dr Paterson, who was very open with them about his views on the matter. His opinions strongly differed from those of Pritchard on the reasons for the demise of both ladies.

After much discussion between Gemmell and McCall, a decision was taken and later that night, as Pritchard stepped down from the last Edinburgh train at Queen Street Railway Station in Glasgow, he was arrested by Mr McCall.

Pritchard protested his innocence loudly and even suggested to McCall alternatives to arresting him, including putting him under house arrest. When this request failed, Pritchard then stated that he was quite ill with a stomach complaint.

McCall was not fooled by Pritchard's pleas; in fact, it was almost as if he had been expecting something of this behaviour from him. McCall listened patiently, then reminded Pritchard that he was still under arrest and led him to the Central Police Station.

Once at the station, Pritchard was placed in McCall's office and he requested that he be provided with some supper. During the course of the meal, Pritchard remained totally calm and confident, even to the point of telling McCall that when the matters were resolved and he was cleared of all suspicion, he intended to sue him for wrongful arrest! Pritchard spent the rest of the night sleeping on a sofa in the office.

The following morning, a message was sent to Edinburgh ordering that the funeral of Mrs Pritchard be stopped. Instead, the body was taken and examined by two eminent pathologists, Drs McLagan and Littlejohn. Their immediate finding, which was conveyed to Superintendant McCall, was that they could find no evidence of death occurring due to natural causes. A further, complete post mortem, including chemical analysis, was arranged .

Pritchard remained at the Central Police Station for the next two days. He constantly maintained his innocence to anyone who would listen and appeared to be more interested in other matters, such as his personal appearance and his meals. He requested that dressing facilities be provided for him and he ate heartily and often, which gave rise to suspicions about his claim of having a stomach illness.

During these two days, Pritchard's house at Sauchiehall Street was being searched thoroughly in an attempt to collect more evidence.

Medicines, bottles and other potions were taken away in large quantities. His servants, friends and acquaintances were also interviewed.

From these interviews, it was discovered that a servant girl in Pritchard's household, Mary Patterson, had, on one occasion, become ill after eating some food that had been intended for Mrs Pritchard. Another servant girl, the aforementioned Mary MacLeod, admitted to having an ongoing sexual relationship with Pritchard right up until the time of his wife's death. She further admitted that during the course of the relationship, she had had an abortion which had been carried out by her lover.

The information provided by Dr Paterson about his antimony poisoning diagnosis of Mrs Pritchard led police to check all chemists in the city. They were successful in locating where Pritchard had purchased his large quantities of drugs. It was learned from the chemist's records that Pritchard had purchased amounts of different poisons which were excessive, even allowing for the fact that he was a dispensing doctor. The police also found the packet of tapioca that Mrs Taylor had eaten from before becoming ill for the first time. Tests showed that the contents contained antimony.

On 28th March, a letter from Dr McLagan stated that Mrs Pritchard's remains were found to have large amounts of antimony present at levels which were more than enough to kill her.

While all other evidence gathered was circumstantial, this is what the police had been waiting for. Pritchard was taken before Sheriff Allison and committed for trial on a charge of murdering his wife.

This development also gave police cause to have Mrs Taylor's body exhumed. Permission was sought for this action and granted. Again, an initial post mortem revealed no natural cause of death. A further investigation was made and antimony was once more found in lethal quantities.

On 20th April, Pritchard was again brought before Sheriff Allison and questioned on this latest development. He refused to answer any questions, on the advice of his solicitor, and he was committed on a second charge of murder.

Due to the complex nature of the case, it was not ready to proceed to trial in time for the Spring Sitting of the Circuit Court (High Court) in Glasgow. Instead, it was scheduled for the Summer Sitting being held in Edinburgh.

Pritchard must have considered this to be fortunate, as every aspect of the case, including evidence and possible motives, had been thoroughly discussed and dissected in the Glasgow tabloids. Such was the interest shown by the public in the fall from grace of a professional man that the chance of having a jury in Glasgow that had not read, heard or been influenced by publicity about the case was almost non-existent.

On 3rd July at the High Court of Justiciary in Parliament Square in Edinburgh, the trial began before the Lord Justice-Clerk, Lord Ardmillan, and Lord Jerviswoode.

Throughout the trial, Pritchard showed no emotion. He appeared calm and unperturbed. His brother Charles Augustus was allowed to sit in the dock with him, presumably to offer some form of comfort, but as the trial was nearing its end, he was instructed to leave on the objection of the Solicitor-General, who was leading the case for the Crown.

For five days, witness after witness gave evidence, with very little in the way of questions being asked of them by the defence. Even the medical evidence was not challenged, when it could so easily have been brought into doubt by the defence side calling their own medical witnesses to refute the claims made, but they could not find even one doctor to testify.

Mary MacLeod, the servant girl, gave damning evidence at the trial that Pritchard had promised to marry her and make her the mistress of the house once he had done away with his wife.

Dr Paterson also gave evidence and was severely reprimanded by the judge for failing to notify the authorities sooner about his suspicions of slow poisoning. The only excuse Paterson could offer for not doing so was 'professional etiquette'.

All the evidence presented was overwhelming and revealed Pritchard as nothing more than a calculating cold-blooded killer, who showed no remorse for his two victims. As a result the verdict was a foregone conclusion.

For the first time since his arrest at the train station, Pritchard found it hard to contain his emotions as the jury returned, after only an hour's deliberations, with two guilty verdicts. Sentence was passed immediately. He was to hang for his crimes.

A large crowd had gathered in Edinburgh's High Street to try to glimpse Pritchard's exit from the courthouse and they had to be held back by a large cordon of police. When he eventually appeared at a side door, the spectators jeered. Pritchard stopped and removed his hat, then slowly and deeply, bowed to the throng before entering the prison van.

During the course of his imprisonment in the cells at the Courthouse in Glasgow, it was revealed that Pritchard had not, as he had claimed, qualified in medicine from King's College, but had purchased

11

his diploma from the University of Erlangen in Germany, which specialised in this type of activity. He had no right to practice as, or even call himself, a Doctor of Medicine in this country.

In the days leading up to his execution, Pritchard made a total of three confessions, two of which were published in daily newspapers. Both these confessions contained a mixture of truth and lies, the most persistent lie being that he was suffering from some form of madness at the time of his crimes.

And so, on the morning of Friday 28th July 1865, with the scaffold in its usual position in Jail Square, just across the street from the Courthouse, facing onto the entrance of the Green, Glasgow's 52nd public execution was soon to take place.

All night long, tens of thousands of people had been gathering in the park. The construction of the scaffold began about 2 a.m. and the echoing noise of many hammers kept up a steady beat. The place had an almost carnival air to it, with side-shows, jugglers, fire-eaters and the like to keep the crowds amused and entertained. It soon developed into a boisterous mass of humanity, which occasionally threatened to get out hand, but as the night progressed and the weather deteriorated, with rain falling incessantly, the crowd became much quieter and settled down to await the morning's events.

As was usual on occasions like this, a great number of religious men took the opportunity to go among the masses and hand out their leaflets proclaiming their 'words of warning'.

The condemned man awoke at 5 a.m. that summer morning and was visited by a minister of religion, who had been a regular attender. During coffee, Pritchard brought up the subject of the second of his three confessions, the one that had not been made public, and in which he had falsely accused Mary MacLeod of committing the two murders. He pleaded that the confession be withheld and destroyed.

After this discussion, Pritchard, as ever, began grooming and dressing himself. He was immaculately attired in the black suit of clothes he had worn throughout his trial and a pair of brown leather boots that he had had specially made. He had never worn them before this day. He had also managed to obtain a pair of new black leather gloves. For some strange reason, Pritchard wore only one glove, on his left hand, the other being tightly held in the grip of his right fist.

By 6 a.m., the rain had stopped and the sun began to shine through. The number of spectators was fewer than anticipated at this time, but from then until the 8 a.m. execution time, all roads leading to the scene were blocked by people eager to witness the grisly procedure.

Every available police officer was called to duty as the crowd swelled to over 80,000.

The gallows, which had the appearance of a large wooden box, stood quietly. In previous executions, a large curtain was usually put in place below the trap door, so that the last agonies of the dying man were hidden from the gaze of the spectators, but not so this time. It had been decreed that, due to the callousness of his crimes and his unrepentant manner, 'no special favour should be allowed to the condemned Pritchard'.

The expression of the day to those sentenced to hang was, 'You'll die facing the Monument', a reference to Nelson's Monument, a tall sandstone column which, even to this day, stands about 300 yards into the Green from the Jail Square entrance. The Monument would be the last thing Pritchard saw before dying, but more importantly, from the spectators' viewpoint, as no curtain was present, they would be able see him too.

Just before 8 a.m., William Calcraft, the executioner, entered the condemned man's cell and Pritchard shook hands with him. Calcraft never uttered a word as he went about his business, securely fastening Pritchard's elbows behind his back with a leather strap.

The procession that accompanied Pritchard then moved from the cells to the courtroom above. Once there, the seven magistrates who had been charged with overseeing the execution asked Pritchard if he wished to make any last statement. After a minute or so of silence, during which time the question was repeated, Pritchard replied in a barely audible voice, 'Simply to acknowledge the justice of my sentence'.

Pritchard was then ushered from the courtroom. He walked with his head slightly raised, as if looking towards heaven. He was then taken down to the underground tunnel that led from the Courthouse to the gallows that awaited across the street.

When he first appeared on the few stairs leading up from the tunnel to the open air of Jail Square, those in the crowd closest to him noted that his eyes were reddened, suggesting that he had been crying. His stride was unaffected though, as he slowly climbed the gibbet steps, stumbling only on the top one, but quickly recovering and taking his place over the trap door without any assistance.

Some of the crowd were now shouting out as the executioner approached and placed the rope around Pritchard's neck and then a white cap over his head. This took slightly more time than expected as Calcraft was having difficulty with Pritchard's long hair and flowing beard.

As Calcraft moved to the side, the spectators immediately fell silent.

13

The hangman was about to remove the bolt that would end life, when he noticed that he had forgotten to secure Pritchard's legs in the same manner as he had his arms. Once he had done this, Calcraft slid back the bolt and the trap door sprung open.

Instantaneously, Pritchard fell towards eternity and the crowd collectively let out a low groan. Calcraft climbed down to below the gallows and pulled on Pritchard's legs, then steadied the body, after which it slowly turned round three times. The glove that he had held throughout in his right hand, fell to the ground. This was the cue for the mass of people to become noisy again and many women screamed loudly, while a large number of the men waved their hats above their heads and cheered.

About a minute after the drop, Pritchard's body stopped twitching. At three minutes after, the fingers of one hand were observed twitching, but they quickly stopped. After five minutes, it was considered that Pritchard was dead and the sentence had been carried out. The majority of spectators began making away from the Green, but it was not until 8.45 a.m. that Pritchard's body was removed from the gallows.

Even then, matters did not run smoothly. As Calcraft loosened the rope and lowered the body towards a coffin which had been placed below to receive it, he miscalculated the weight and allowed the body to drop at speed, which forced the bottom out of the casket. Pritchard's body was pulled up again while joiners were summoned to repair the damage. After a delay of some ten minutes while this was carried out, Pritchard's body was eventually placed in the coffin and taken back to the Courthouse.

Within two hours of the execution, the large crowd had all dispersed. Hutchestown Bridge was re-opened to traffic and the barricades in front of the Courthouse had all been removed. The clothing stalls of the nearby Paddy's Market were open for business as if nothing had happened.

As Pritchard's body lay in the Courthouse, a number of strange events took place. All his hair and beard were shaved off in order that Alexander Stewart of the Edinburgh Phrenological Society could take a plaster cast of his head and face. They also took casts of his hands and feet! The presiding magistrates had ordered that all the shaven hair be burned.

However, Pritchard's eldest daughter had previously written to the governor of the prison and asked that she be given a lock of her father's hair as a keepsake. This request had been agreed to, but when the hair was called for to be handed over, it was alleged that it had all been destroyed.

Then it was found that Calcraft, the hangman, somewhat ghoulishly was in possession of the criminal's hair and he was instructed to hand it over. Calcraft was reluctant to comply with this order and he had to be strongly persuaded otherwise.

About 1 p.m. that day, Pritchard's body, dressed in the clothes he had worn on the scaffold, was buried. A grave had been dug within the yard of the Courthouse prison and the short service was attended by only a small number of officials, one of them being Superintendant McCall. No member of Pritchard's family was present. The stone that covered his final resting place bore the simple inscription, 'E.W.P. 1865'.

Glasgow's last public execution had drawn to a close. All future executions took place behind closed doors, first at Duke Street Prison and thereafter at Barlinnie Prison.

For one hundred and twenty years, no one thought there was any mystery surrounding the life and times of 'Dr' Edward Pritchard, until the day in 1985 when the workman found the boots and hair hidden in the tunnel wall.

Now that the mystery as to the question of who had been the original owner of both these items has been answered, it still remains to discover who placed them there and why?

The answer to the first part of the remaining question is that William Calcraft, the executioner, placed them in the secret niche. Calcraft was responsible for Pritchard's body until he returned it to the Courthouse and handed it over to the authorities. However, on this occasion, he had additional duties inasmuch as he had to shave the head and beard of Pritchard to make it ready for the plaster moulds to be taken. He also had to remove the boots from the body to allow casts to be obtained of the feet. After this had been done, he was further charged with placing the body in the coffin to await burial. At this point, his duties were complete and he could hand the body over to those responsible for the interment.

Research into this matter reveals that Calcraft was the regular executioner, employed by the authorities over a great many years, although he had the reputation of being fairly haphazard in his methods of carrying out his duties. At every execution he presided over, Calcraft always took a memento of the occasion, and without exception, it was a personal item of the condemned man. The authorities were aware of this but they never objected to the practice, probably because it was always difficult to fill the post of executioner and get someone who was reasonably competent at the same time.

Following the argument over the demand made for Pritchard's hair, it is almost certain that Calcraft decided to hide his gruesome trophies, lest he was seen with them and ordered to hand them over too. He placed them in their hiding place, intending to uplift them at the next execution he was in charge of, once all the outcry over the Pritchard affair had been forgotten about.

He was not to know that later that same year, the decision would be taken not to have any more public executions, and further, that due to his dishonest behaviour at the Pritchard hanging, he would never be employed again in Glasgow as a hangman!

So, Calcraft had no way of getting back into the tunnel to remove his mementoes. No one but he knew they were there and there is no way he was going to reveal their existence, so bringing more disrepute on himself. Calcraft remained silent and the boots and hair of Pritchard remained hidden in the tunnel until their accidental discovery.

Calcraft, in later years, turned into a bitter man, fond of regularly taking an excessive amount to drink, after which he would voice his opinions on both the authorities and Pritchard, each of whom he held equally responsible for his unemployed state. Occasionally, he supplemented his income by selling off some of the articles he had taken from those he had executed.

In recent years the Saltmarket Courthouse has undergone a massive expansion programme with the addition of another four courtrooms in an extension built at the rear of the original building. The Courthouse is next to where the grave of Pritchard was sited, along with others who were executed in previous years. It is probable that the graves have now been covered over with concrete for all time. There is no information about what has happened to Pritchard's boots and hair since 1985!

Once last piece of information. Rumour has it that the Courthouse had two tunnels, one of which we have just read about and another, longer one, under the length of the Saltmarket, leading all the way to the Tollbooth at Glasgow Cross. The Tollbooth was used as a prison and a place of execution prior to the Courthouse being built. If the rumours are true, what mysteries and secrets might this tunnel hold?

Two
THE EDINBURGH BUSHRANGERS

In the darkness of a cold winter evening on Friday 4th February 1881, two poorly dressed men stood huddled against the side of an Edinburgh building. They were sheltering from the occasional flurries of snow, borne on a biting wind that cut into them at every blast. Who these men were and the crimes they had committed before this night has remained a mystery.

Even as they shivered, their eyes darted continuously up and down the deserted thoroughfare, searching for their quarry. They had been loitering in the shadows of the city's Queensferry Road for over an hour, and just before 6 p.m. their gaze settled on a lone pedestrian, Robert Veitch, a 26-year-old commercial traveller, who was making his way along the street, stooped and muffled against the elements.

Veitch had almost reached his destination of Dean Park Farm, where his father was manager, when the two men stepped out of the shadows and barred his way. Before he could utter a word, one of the men shouted 'Your money or your life!'. Although totally surprised by both the appearance of the men and their demand, Veitch, in an instinctive response, bravely began to set about the pair with his rolled-up umbrella. It was now the turn of the would-be robbers to be surprised as the blows rained down on them.

The attack did not last long though, as the umbrella broke. Veitch seized the chance to escape and ran to his home. Once there, he enlisted the help of his father and younger sister Emily, and the three of them ran out into the street to confront the two attackers. Prior to leaving the house, Veitch armed himself with a heavy walking stick.

17

By the time they arrived back at the scene, the highwaymen had made off. They were quickly spotted in the distance further down Belford Road near to Ravelston Place. The Veitchs ran and caught up with the men and detained them, telling them that they were now to go to the local police station. The strangers, at this mention of police, turned menacingly, and Robert Veitch, fearing the worst again, struck one of the men a heavy pre-emptive blow on the head with his stick.

This action was the final catalyst and both strangers produced revolvers from within their jackets and began firing at all members of the family. Robert was shot twice in the head and fell to the ground immediately. His sister was struck in the head and leg and she too was knocked to the pavement. Mr Veitch senior had a narrow escape from injury which he only later discovered. A bullet from one of the pistols passed through his waistcoat, tearing a hole in his shirt but not injuring him.

Both robbers ran off together, leaving Veitch senior to flag down a passing vehicle, load his injured son and daughter into it and convey them the short distance home. Once there, a neighbour, alerted by the volley of shots, hurriedly made his way to Stockbridge Police Station to raise the alarm.

Having been made aware of the events, the police treated the incident so seriously that they used their newly installed telephone system to inform their Chief Constable, who instructed that a squad of at least 60 officers should be formed. Messages were sent to the homes of off-duty constables, telling them to report for duty immediately.

In the meantime, Robert and Emily Veitch had been removed to the local infirmary. Robert had lost almost all of his right ear, the bullet having torn it away, while the other had entered his neck. His sister was more seriously injured by a bullet that entered her neck just below her right ear, travelled up through her throat and exited out of her left cheek. Her jaw was broken in many places as a result. The second shot entered her hip, fracturing her pelvis.

As the police task force assembled, the two would-be robbers found themselves in the area of Murrayfield in the west of the city. About 8.30 p.m., they accosted James Dick, a visitor from Dalry in Ayrshire, while he was walking with his girlfriend in the street. This time the robbers took no chances as one of them immediately struck him on the head with his pistol, then thrust it into his face, followed closely with the same demand as before, 'Your money or your life!'.

Dick fumbled in his pockets and produced coins totalling about four shillings. After he handed this over, the highwaymen expressed their severe displeasure with the haul and ordered Dick to hand over his gold watch. As he began to comply, Dick saw that both men were constantly looking around and at one point, neither was watching him.

He took the opportunity and ran off. Surprisingly, no shots were fired at him and he never stopped running until he reached Coltbridge Police Station, which was unfortunately closed. Dick regained his breath and began walking towards the city centre. As he was doing so, he realised for the first time that he had lost his hat, which was especially upsetting as it was quite new.

Soon, Dick came upon a patrolling policeman and related the tale of his assault. He was escorted to Stockbridge Police Station where he was interviewed by the Chief Constable, who had arrived and taken charge of the investigation. The incidents were something totally new for the police. While street robberies were an occasional crime, the use of firearms was almost unheard of in Victorian times.

The two highway robbers had, by now, caught a tram into the city centre. The smaller of the two was wearing Dick's hat, his own having been crushed earlier when Veitch had hit him over the head. After arriving in the city centre about 9 p.m., they again faded into the shadows, only to reappear a short time later in Bonnington Road.

They had spied what they considered to be a chance to make some easy money when they came across a baker's van sitting quietly at the pavement edge. They quickly reached up and pulled the driver from the open seat, throwing him onto the roadway. One robber sat astride the driver's chest and put the muzzle of his pistol under the frightened man's chin, ordering him to remain calm and not to struggle. A knife was produced and the leather straps holding his money pouch were cut. As quietly as they had appeared, so they disappeared into the darkness with the driver's takings.

By now, the city's police force was on red alert. Reports of sightings, real or imaginary, of the two robbers were coming in but it was not until around midnight that a police officer got a close look at the two outlaws for the first time.

Sergeants William Arnott and Donald Reid were on duty at Leith Docks, manning the wooden hut that served as a police office at the entrance to the docks in Dock Place. They were being especially vigilant, not because they were aware of events in other parts of the city, but mainly as a result of an earlier incident. On the previous Wednesday, two men had been disturbed attempting to break into the Queen's

19

Store, which was sited behind the Customs House, and it was thought then that they might return to complete the job on another night.

Around midnight, the two officers were on their rounds when they observed two shadowy figures hugging the walls of the Queen's Store and occasionally peering in the windows. Creeping up on them, the officers surprised the men and detained them. When asked their business, the men replied that they were seamen trying to find their way back to their ship. When pressed further, they named the vessel, but the sergeants immediately realised that the ship did not exist.

This was enough for the officers and the men were told to accompany them to the nearby police office at the dock gates. Although reluctant, the men did not protest too much as both were taken by the arm and began walking towards the police hut.

Just prior to turning the corner into Dock Place, the pair of robbers glanced towards at each other and simultaneously stepped to opposite sides. The policemen had seen the exchanged looks, even in the darkness, but in the split second that it took to register that something was about to happen, it had already occurred.

Both robbers produced revolvers from their hiding places and immediately began firing continuously at the officers. One of the first bullets hit Sergenat Arnott at the side of the head, just below his left ear, tearing through his neck and out again above his shoulder blades. He was thrown to the ground with the force of the bullet.

Sergeant Reid was shot in the back and fell onto one knee. At this point, both gunmen ran off, but were pursued by the injured Reid. As all three ran into Commercial Road, the shrill screams of Arnott's police whistle pierced the night air in alarm.

Reid, who was losing a large amount of blood from his wound, was, as a result, slowing in his pursuit of his assailants. A young constable named Cameron, alerted by Arnott's whistle, arrived in Commercial Street and gave chase to the fleeing criminals. However, he stopped momentarily when Reid stumbled to a halt in front of him, and when he resumed the hunt, discovered that his quarry had disappeared from view.

Two constables, Nicolson and Byrne, were on duty at the railway gates opposite Leith Citadel and saw the gunmen running past. The officers called on the men to stop and as they approached found themselves under fire from a volley of pistol shots. Nicolson collected a bullet in the knee, but he and his colleague began chasing the men. Constable McConville, who was the local beat officer, had been alerted by both the whistle and the gunshots and joined his fellow officers in the chase.

Throughout the chase, the gunmen continually turned and fired their revolvers at their pursuers, but fortunately no shots hit the target. At this point, either by agreement or accident, the fleeing gunmen split up and ran in different directions. One fled into Admiralty Street, which in the darkness appeared to him to be a dead-end. In reality it was not. However, as he turned to retrace his steps, he was confronted by the uniform of McConville, who had followed him.

The cornered man took aim with his pistol and fired at the policeman, but missed. The gunman then ran across the street, put his back against the wall and fired again. Once more he missed. McConville moved forward, slowly advancing on the man with his hand outstretched for the gun to be given up. Yet again, the gunman fired and this time McConville felt the heat as the bullet whistled past his ear! As the officer got close enough almost to make a grab for the pistol, the gunman took two steps back, jammed the barrel of the revolver into his own mouth and pulled the trigger. The top of his head flew off in the explosion and the brick wall behind was splattered with blood as his lifeless body crumpled to the ground.

The second gunman was still being pursued by Nicolson, Byrne and Cameron. By now, he was beginning to tire and the officers were getting closer to him, and although he continued to turn and aim his pistol at them and pull the trigger, it failed to fire.

Exhausted, the gunman suddenly stopped and turned to face his pursuers. As they slowed and closed on him, he put the revolver in his mouth and pulled the trigger, but it failed to fire. He snatched at the trigger several times more, but on each occasion it mis-fired. The gunman released his grip on the weapon and handed it to the officers, saying, 'You had better take the bloody thing. It has deserted me at the last moment. If it had done its duty, like my chum's did, I would be as far out of your reach as he is now'.

The officers marched their captive back to Admiralty Street and met their colleague McConville. As the prisoner stood quietly, looking down at his dead companion, he was heard to whisper, 'I wish I was beside him'. James Dick's almost-new hat lay discarded in the gutter, next to the body.

All the injured police officers and the dead gunman were conveyed to Leith Infirmary. One, Sergeant Arnott, was in a particularly bad way and required immediate surgery to his wounds.

The captured gunman was taken to Leith Police headquarters and when asked to state his name, said it was James Grant. He further stated that his dead colleague was called Frank Seymour.

Early on Saturday morning, Grant appeared in front of Bailie Wilkie, who in turn remitted him to Edinburgh Sheriff Court on charges of discharging a firearm with intent to murder. Later, in the afternoon, Grant made a special appearance at this Court, before Sheriff Hamilton, and it is alleged that during these proceedings, the prisoner made 'various rather important statements'. Unfortunately, these statements have not survived, but it is almost certain that they were a repeat of those made to police investigators during the night in the aftermath of the shootings.

When Grant was interviewed at length, he stated that the names he had provided to the police for both himself and his dead companion were false, and further, that he would soon confess to a serious crime that either he or he and his friend had committed. Whether that crime had occurred in Scotland or abroad, he never mentioned.

In the light of this new information, the body of gunman Frank Seymour was removed from the Infirmary and taken to police headquarters in Leith, where it was examined in great detail by the police surgeon, Dr Garland. He was under instructions to look for the smallest mark that might assist in identifying the deceased.

The doctor noted that on the side of Seymour's head was a fairly large, fresh cut and put this injury down to the occasion when Robert Veitch struck one of his attackers with the heavy stick. Garland then discovered two scars on the chest of the dead man, one on each breast. He concluded that they were old gunshot wounds. Photographs of Seymour, as he lay on the marble slab, were taken and dispatched to Scotland Yard, along with those taken of Grant, in an effort to establish their true identities.

The revolvers used by both men had been recovered and examined. They were found to be of a type known as English or British 'Bulldog' make and to have the capacity to fire six shots. Enquiries discovered that this type of weapon was popular in Australia and America.

Grant and Seymour's lodgings above a coffee shop in the city's Old Town area were searched for further evidence. All that was discovered was that they shared a tiny room together. There was not even a single personal belonging found in the room.

After his court appearance and over the course of the weekend, Grant was further interviewed, and during one of these sessions, he admitted that both he and Seymour had recently arrived in the UK aboard a vessel called the *Melbourne*. A check revealed that a vessel of

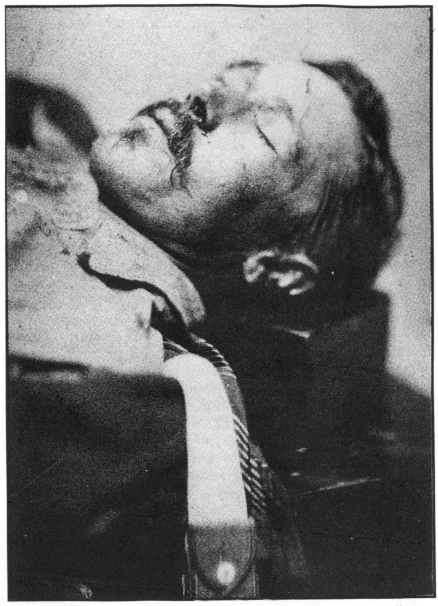

Photograph of Frank Seymour lying on a mortuary slab, taken in an effort to identify him (Courtesy of the Keeper of the Records of Scotland)

that name had arrived at Tilbury Docks, London, on 31st January 1881.

Officers from Scotland Yard were sent to interview the captain, and when shown the photographs, he identified Grant as James

Harnett and Seymour as William Smith. Both had been crew members, having signed on as able seamen prior to the vessel leaving its namesake port of Melbourne, Victoria, in November 1880 for the trip to London.

The captain added that he had had no trouble from either man during the trip and that they appeared to be in the company of a third man called William Harrison. All three jumped ship as soon as it berthed at Tilbury.

All of this circumstantial evidence led the authorities, and the press, to believe that Grant (Harnett) and Seymour (Smith) were fleeing members of an Australian gang of outlaws, known throughout the world as 'Ned Kelly's Gang'. This myth has been perpetuated right up until the present day, with occasional articles on the subject being published. It is not hard to see the reasons why.

In Australia, Edward 'Ned' Kelly became infamous in the state of Victoria around the middle of 1878. A newly installed constable attempted to arrest Ned's brother for a minor offence, got injured in the process and later claimed that it was Ned who had shot him. The next day, Ned's mother, his brother-in-law and a neighbour were arrested for their non-existent part in the incident. Mrs Kelly was sent to prison for three years, while the other two received six-year sentences. Ned had a reward of £100 placed on his head.

As a direct consequence of this mistreatment of his family, Ned and his brother Dan went on the run. They were joined by two friends, Steve Hart and Joe Byrne, and this was the beginning of the 'Kelly Gang'. Later that same year, they ambushed a police patrol that was hunting them, killing three, with the fourth escaping to tell the authorities. This incident alone increased the reward money to £500.

It is alleged that 'Ned Kelly and his gang never robbed a woman or harmed a poor man. They were never highwaymen like the old-fashioned bushrangers'. This would appear to be confirmed by the list of crimes they actually committed. Their 'vendetta' was aimed at the Government and its employees.

The Kelly Gang then carried out two bank robberies in the space of two months, one at Euroa, and the other at Jerilderie, across the border in New South Wales. In all, these raids netted just over £4,000. By the end of the second robbery, the rewards offered on each member of the gang stood at £2,000. For 16 months after the last bank raid, nothing was seen or heard of the Kelly Gang, as they laid low to avoid the outcry and massive searches now going on in two states.

On 27th June 1880, they rode to Glenrowan, a small town north of Melbourne. Once there, they took over a hotel and imprisoned about 30 of the townsfolk in it but it was all part of a daring plan.

One of the gang, Joe Byrne, had earlier in the day shot and killed a friend of his, who had been informing on the gang to the police. The gang knew this murder would be reported to the authorities, and to make doubly sure that it would, the crime was carried out in full view of four police constables, who had been assigned to guard the informant.

When news of the murder reached the police, a squad of 30 or more officers were put on a special train and began making for Glenrowan. However, this is exactly what Ned Kelly had hoped would happen and he forced some railway workers to tear up the tracks just south of the town. The idea was to wreck the train, kill the police detachment and then drive the engine back down the line and rob the bank at a place called Benalla.

Unfortunately, being confined to the town hotel led to the gang partaking of too much alcohol from the bar, eventually getting drunk and falling asleep. One of the detained townspeople, the schoolmaster Thomas Curnow, escaped and managed to flag down the train before it ran out of track.

As darkness prevailed, it was decided to use it as cover and the police team stormed the hotel. Kelly's Gang, having heard the train's whistle, were waiting for them, all dressed in makeshift armour and standing out in front of the hotel. A fierce gun battle took place in the moonlight.

Ned, wearing a cylindrical metal headpiece, and metal plates held together with leather straps covering his front and back, was shot three times, once each in the hand, arm and foot. He managed to limp away in the darkness and confusion to lie low in the bush. The other three were forced to retreat into the hotel by the sheer ferocity of the superior firepower.

A couple of hours later, Joe Byrne was shot dead by a police marksman as he stood at the bar of the hotel. As dawn broke about 7 a.m., the police squad now numbered 50, more having arrived from nearby towns during the night. The heat of the early morning sun sucked the overnight moisture from the earth, creating a mist. Out of it loomed Ned Kelly, still wearing his armour and firing at the police. A number of shots, intelligently aimed only at his legs, brought him down and he was eventually arrested.

For the next three hours, bullets rained on the hotel from every direction, until some of the imprisoned townspeople appeared from within. Within five minutes, all the hostages, with the exception of one who had been caught in the crossfire and injured, were now free. Only Dan Kelly, Hart and the already dead Byrne remained within.

The shooting began again and went on until 3 p.m., when a policeman set fire to the wooden building. One of the onlookers, a priest, entered the burning hotel and after a few minutes came out to say that all three were now dead. Some policemen entered but because of the intensity of the blaze, could only bring out one corpse, that of Byrne.

When the fire had extinguished itself, the two remaining corpses of Kelly and Hart were removed. They were burned beyond recognition but there was no doubt as to their identities and they were handed over to relatives for immediate burial. Neither had bullet wounds on them and it is thought they had swallowed poison rather than be taken alive.

Ned Kelly stood trial at Melbourne, was found guilty of all the crimes he was charged with and hanged in the town's jail on 11th November 1880. It is almost a certainty that Grant and Seymour were among the thousands in the crowds that thronged Melbourne for Kelly's date with the hangman. After that, they departed aboard the *Melbourne*, using the false names Harnett and Smith, for both were criminals in their own right. They were thieves and fraudsters and had previous dealings with the Australian courts in relation to these crimes. There is evidence to suggest that Seymour had a warrant out for his arrest at the time of the ship's departure, hence the need for a new identity. Far from the names James Grant and Frank Seymour being aliases, these were their real names.

There is absolutely no doubt that the two Edinburgh bushrangers were not part of Kelly's gang, who were now all dead. Nor were Grant and Seymour among a group of 26 of Kelly's closest sympathisers who were arrested between January and March 1879 and thrown into prison without charge in an attempt to flush the gang from their hide-out.

Grant spent three months in Calton Jail awaiting his trial and was watched 24 hours a day by at least one prison warder and sometimes two as he was considered to be a suicide risk. He never did reveal to the police any serious crimes committed either here or abroad. After being legally advised, he probably decided to keep quiet because none of the victims of his and Seymour's night of lawlessness had died as a result, thanks mainly to the skills of the hospital staff.

Grant went on trial at Edinburgh High Court on 24th May 1881. The trial lasted a mere six hours, during which time he never uttered a word. It was not until he had been found guilty and Lord Young had sentenced him to 14 years penal servitude, that an outburst came from the prisoner in the dock. He stood up and said, 'My Lord, I wish you had brought in capital punishment because I intended to commit murder that night. I do not wish to live'.

So what were the reasons for the violent outrages committed that cold February night? The answers are simply that Grant and Seymour were penniless and had no clothing suitable for a Scottish winter. Perhaps they thought that in a large city such as Edinburgh, with an unarmed police force, they could shoot and steal their way to providing themselves with an income. They were what Kelly and his gang had not been—old fashioned highwaymen, or as Australians preferred to call them, bushrangers. Ned Kelly would never have tolerated them—if indeed, he ever knew them!

Three
THE DUNDEE 'RIPPER'?

The greatest mystery of Victorian times was undoubtedly that surrounding the identity of the killer who prowled London's dark alleys and who became known all over the world as 'Jack the Ripper'.

From August to November 1888, five murders occurred in the east end area of Whitechapel in London in which five women, four of them prostitutes, were killed and mutilated. As suddenly as these murders started, so they ended and this led to another mystery. Why did the killings stop?

Since that time and right up until the present day, countless theories and opinions have been published in hundreds of books on the subject of who the murderer might have been and why he stopped when he did. Could the murderer have died? Could he (or she, as some theories suggest) have been discovered and stopped from carrying out any more foul deeds? Or could the murderer simply have moved away from the area, perhaps to begin again somewhere else?

In 1988, on the centenary of the crimes, a new name was put forward for the first time as a possible identity for the Ripper, and such was the evidence that accompanied it, his name was added to the ever growing list of suspects, which now numbers almost 150, and range in diversity from a deranged member of the Royal Family to an avenging midwife! The name of this new suspect was William Henry Bury.

Bury was not a Londoner, having been born in Wolverhampton in 1859. However, after reaching 18 years of age, he decided, like many others, to seek his fortune in the capital. Not much is known of him in the years between arriving in London and April 1888, when he met and married Ellen Elliot, who was an occasional servant girl in

28

the house of James Martin in Bromley in Kent. Martin also employed Bury as a sand and sawdust seller.

Bury was an alcoholic, who, when drunk, had a violent temper. He would spend all of his wages, and, on occasion, some of his employer's takings, on getting blind drunk, and this caused numerous arguments between his wife and himself, which usually ended in Mrs Bury being on the receiving end of a beating.

When they married, the Burys took lodgings with an Elizabeth Haynes in Swaton Road, Bow in London's East End. On the Saturday after the ceremony, Haynes heard screams from her lodger's bedroom and on entering, discovered Bury standing over his wife, who had been knocked to the floor. He was threatening to stab her with a large knife he held in his hand.

Haynes stated that she was going to fetch the police, but Bury persuaded her otherwise, handing the knife over to her and promising not to repeat his behaviour. After he left the house to calm down, Mrs Bury told Haynes that the argument flared when she refused to give him money to go drinking.

Fortunately for Bury, his wife had a small inheritance, in the form of shares, left to her by an aunt who had died seven years previously. With very little money coming in due to his drinking and because his wife was only employed part-time, the shares were cashed in in June of that year and the sum of almost £200 was raised from their sale.

In August, the Burys vacated their lodgings, saying that they were moving to Wolverhampton. However, this was a lie, probably because Bury detested Haynes, who, after the earlier incident, made sure that his wife came to no harm at his hands. They remained in the area, renting rooms at 11 Blackthorn Street, Bow. They stayed there only until December, when they moved again, this time to 3 Spanby Road, Bow. Hardly a month had passed, when they paid a visit to Mrs Bury's married sister, Margaret Corney. During the visit, William Bury stated that they were moving again, this time to Dundee, where he said he had secured jobs for them both for the next seven years with a firm involved in the jute industry.

The reason for this sudden decision to uproot themselves from the area they knew so well, and where they had friends and relatives, is difficult to understand until it is learned that Bury had been sacked by Mr Martin for spending the takings on alcohol once too often. He was, no doubt, deep in debt for drink consumed and rent owed.

Far from being pleased, Mrs Corney knew that her sister was regularly beaten by her husband and the money from the sale of the shares was almost gone, the majority of it spent by Bury on his two and three day long drinking binges. Corney implored her sister to leave her husband, but she would not agree to it.

On Saturday 19th January 1889, the Burys departed London from the docks at Gravesend aboard the steamer *Cambria*, arriving in Dundee the following evening. After spending Sunday night on board, they walked down the gangway and into the city. Their first priority was to find a place to stay.

As they trudged through the streets on a cold and bitter winter day, Bury was having difficulty carrying a large white wooden box he had had specially made in London. It contained all their personal belongings. Eventually, almost at the end of the day, they found a room to rent at the house of Mrs Robertson at 43 Union Street in the city.

Within two days of their arrival, and probably at his wife's insistence, Bury was forced to attempt to find some employment. Somewhat strangely, Bury called on Edward Gough, the minister of St Paul's Episcopal Church, and asked for his help in finding employment. Gough suggested that work in the shipyards might be the answer and said that he would do what he could to help.

The Burys lodged with Mrs Robertson for just over a week. The rent was eight shillings a week and Bury thought that it was too expensive. During this time, he visited an estate agents in the Cowgate and enquired about two-roomed houses for lease. He was given keys to view one such property at 113 Princes Street, a basement flat under a shop. However, he retained the keys and he and his wife immediately moved out of their lodgings with Mrs Robertson and into their new accommodation. That he did not intend to pay any rent only made it more attractive.

The next two weeks were spent visiting different public houses in the city. Bury usually went on these drinking sprees alone, leaving his wife to her own devices. She made friends with Marjory Smith, who was the proprietor of the shop above the flat. When Mrs Smith asked why they had come to Dundee, Mrs Bury replied that her husband was prone to staying out late with his drinking friends in London and she thought the change of locale would alter his errant ways. However, it did not and Bury made new friends on his marathon drinking sessions. One of these was Alexander Patterson, owner of a public house only yards from Bury's new home.

On Monday night, 4th February, the Bury's paid a visit to a pub and left around closing time. As usual, Bury was drunk, but his wife appeared reasonably sober. On his returning to their home, an argument developed to such an extent that one later witness, David Duncan, who lived at 101 Princes Street, about 20 yards away across the communal back gardens, heard three loud screams between 2 and 3 a.m. on the Tuesday morning. The screams were of such intensity that Duncan got up from his bed and listened for half an hour. He felt sure the screams had come from the direction of Bury's home, but he heard nothing further to convince him completely of that.

For the next five days, Bury continued as he had done before. He was a constant fixture in Patterson's pub and occasionally his wife's name cropped up in conversation. Bury calmly stated that she was unwell and remained at home.

In the early evening of Sunday 10th February, Bury walked into the Central Police Office in Bell Street, Dundee and asked to speak with the officer in charge as he had some important information. Lieutenant Parr, the most senior officer on duty at the time, took Bury to a side-room and as soon as they entered, Bury is alleged to have said, 'I'm Jack the Ripper' or 'I'm a Jack the Ripper'. Unfortunately, before Parr could question him on this remark, Bury, in an excited state, began rambling on about his wife having committed suicide. Parr eventually calmed him down and the story unfolded.

Bury stated that on the previous Monday night, he and his wife had both been drinking. He went to his bed drunk and when he awoke the following morning, found his wife dead on the floor with a rope around her neck. Inexplicably, he then mutilated her body with a knife and squeezed it into the wooden packing case which held their belongings. He had lived with his thoughts of this terrible deed, and the dead body, for five days and now he wished to clear his conscience.

Bury was detained and Lieutenant David Lamb, head of the C.I.D., was despatched to Princes Street to check on this story. The front room was found to be devoid of furniture, but on entering the rear room, he was confronted by the large wooden box sitting in the middle of the floor. He examined the crate and found that two boards on the top were loose. Having prised them open, Lamb saw a quantity of bed clothing. He removed them and to his horror was confronted by the legs and feet of a naked body.

Recovering from his shock, Lamb instructed the junior detective with him to go and fetch the police surgeon, Dr Templeman. When the doctor attended, the body was examined further. It was found to be lying on its back, but was doubled up due to the size of the crate.

31

In order for the corpse to fit in the box, both legs were folded over and one had been broken to make it easier. The left leg was lying across the body diagonally, the foot resting on the right shoulder, while the right leg was broken just below the knee.

Although this in itself was a gruesome sight, worse was to follow. As the body was being removed from the packing case, it was noticed that there were a large number of cuts and slashes across the stomach of Mrs Bury. From one of these wounds, the bowels and intestines fell out and spilled into the box and onto the floor.

After the body was laid out on the floor, the bruising around the neck was clearly visible. A complete and thorough search was made of the room and a blood-stained knife was found next to the window. A piece of cord, which had hair entwined in it, was also recovered nearby. The ashes in the fireplace grate were sifted through and what appeared to be small fragments of burned cloth were discovered.

A preliminary examination by Templeman concluded that death was due to a combination of strangulation and stabbing. The body was then removed to the mortuary for a full post mortem.

Meantime, Lieutenant Lamb was searching the immediate area for clues and it is alleged he came upon two messages, written in chalk and scrawled on the back door and walls of the property. They read, 'Jack Ripper is at the back of this door' and 'Jack Ripper is in this sellar'. Lamb assumed that both scrawls had been written by children and thought no more about it.

Nonetheless, the Metropolitan Police were informed of Bury's arrest and the nature of his crime. Surprisingly, the English force showed no interest in the matter whatsoever, and, at first, failed even to respond to requests for information on Bury's past history and movements.

Bury was interviewed at length, but he seemed to be much calmer than he had been at the first instance. He continually assured the police that his wife had committed suicide! He was taken before the local police court and formally charged with murder and remanded in prison custody. His clothes had, in the interval, been taken from him, and he appeared somewhat dishevelled in the alternative clothing provided. It was badly fitting, which is not surprising considering that he was a small thin man, weighing just over 9 stones and only 5" 2' in height.

On 28th March 1889, Bury went on trial at the High Court in Dundee. The case caused much interest in the local population as such a horrific murder had never before been committed within their boundaries. The public benches of the court were overflowing with those anxious to catch a glimpse of the proceedings as Bury was brought up from the cells below and entered a plea of Not Guilty.

The court heard from a number of witnesses, including Bury's former employer, Mr Martin, and Mrs Bury's share broker. One prosecution witness, D. R. Malcolm, partner in merchants Malcolm Ogilvy and Co., Dundee, was shown a piece of paper which was alleged to be a contract between his firm and the accused Bury. It said that Bury was to be employed for a period of seven years and would be paid £2 per week. If his wife also wished to work, she was to receive £1 a week. Malcolm stated that the agreement was nothing other than a forgery.

The medical evidence then took up the remainder of the trial and it held the packed galleries spellbound. Dr Templeman explained that he had carried out a post mortem on Mrs Bury and that in addition to the rope marks and stab wounds, he found a number of bruises. In particular, there was one on the side of her head. He considered the blow that had caused it would have been severe enough to render her unconscious. The rope was then placed around her neck and she was stabbed and mutilated before dying of strangulation.

This lurid description of the sequence of events caused murmurs of shock and much discussion among the onlookers. After a minute or so, and much hammering of his gavel, Lord Young demanded order to be restored.

Templeman's findings were corroborated by Dr Stalker and eminent Edinburgh pathologist Dr Littlejohn, a veteran of many a Scottish murder case. Littlejohn also informed the court that he had measured the wounds on the stomach at just over 26 inches in total. On completing his evidence, the case for the Crown closed.

The defence counsel, Mr Hay Q.C., then called on his medical witnesses, Drs Lennox and Kinnear, in an effort to refute the evidence already presented. Both doctors' testimony was similar to that led by the Crown but with two exceptions. They contended that the strangulation was suicidal and that the stab wounds had been inflicted only after death. Both were cross-examined in great detail, during which Kinnear was forced to disclose that he had only qualified as a doctor five months previously and that he had never before heard of a case of suicide where strangulation was the method employed, let alone seen one.

By the time the defence had finished, it was 7 p.m. Lord Young informed the jury members that they had to make a decision whether to continue that night or instead, be locked up overnight and conclude the following day. After a quick consultation, they decided to continue. For the next three hours they listened intently to the eloquent speeches on behalf of the prosecution and defence and the summing-up and charge of the judge. Not until just after 10 p.m. were they allowed to retire to consider their verdict.

After only twenty minutes' absence, the jury returned and informed the hushed court that they had unanimously found Bury guilty of murder, but then sensationally recommended to the judge that mercy be shown to him. Once again, the public benches erupted and shouts and whistles of derision, aimed at the jury, echoed around the room.

After the disturbance subsided, the judge quizzed the jury foreman as to why they were suggesting Bury receive mercy and he replied that it was due to the conflicting medical evidence. Lord Young forcibly told the jury that they had no grounds for making this recommendation and that they would now have to go to the jury room again to reconsider their position on the initial verdict. The defence team thought that this was a good omen as some doubt was obviously present in the minds of the jurors. They hoped for a positive result.

This time the jury were absent only five minutes before returning, again with a unanimous verdict of guilty. For the third time, the galleries exploded in a sea of noise, only on this occasion with loud cheering and applause. There was no need for shouts for order to be restored as the usher of the court moved behind Lord Young and placed a black handkerchief on his head. The excited spectators quietened immediately to hear the only sentence possible being handed down. Bury was to hang.

Although it was by now 11 p.m., the court having sat continuously for thirteen hours, over 5,000 people waited in the streets surrounding the courthouse to hear the verdict. When word filtered through to them what it was, a spontaneous cheer erupted, so loud that it is said everyone in Dundee heard it!

The sentence of death was due to be carried out on 24th April at Dundee Prison. In the three weeks between the end of the trial and this date, Bury was visited daily by the Rev. Gough, who attended to his spiritual needs. An appeal for a reprieve was also set in motion.

Bury appeared to be unconcerned about his approaching fate, eating heartily and sleeping soundly, until on Monday 22nd April, he was taken before the prison governor and told that his appeal for mercy had failed. That night, he broke down in his cell and wept uncontrollably for hours..

As morning broke on his appointed day with the hangman, Bury rose about 5 a.m. and consumed the breakfast provided for him. He then sat back and lit a cigarette, breaking the silence in the room by saying to one of the warders, 'This is my last morning on Earth. I freely forgive all who gave false evidence against me'.

Just after 7 a.m., as was usual practice in these proceedings, the condemned man was taken before an assembly of local magistrates, whose collective duty was to ensure that the sentence of the court was carried out correctly. Bury was asked if he wished to make any statement, but he hung his head and remained silent.

As Bury stood there with his head bowed, the executioner Berry and his assistant Scott quietly moved behind the prisoner and pinioned his arms to his sides, using a leather thong hooked around his elbows. Not one person in the room spoke and some looked away as the inevitable procedure began.

Bury was then taken from the room and ushered down the eerily quiet corridors of the prison towards his cell. Once there, he met the Rev. Gough, who began reciting passages from the open bible in his hands. Occasionally, Bury could be heard to say something in quiet response to the verses.

As the town clock began tolling the hour set for the execution, the procession moved from the condemned cell and made its way the forty or so yards to the site of the gallows, the Rev. Gough still reciting and Bury responding. At almost halfway, the entourage stopped and the executioner stepped forward and removed Bury's collar and tie and somewhat callously threw it onto the floor. Almost in the same movement, he placed a white cap over Bury's head and face. The procession then continued with Bury having to be led by the hangman.

Once on the gibbet platform, Bury's legs were quickly shackled and the noose adjusted around his neck. As the hangman stepped back from doing this and without any further ceremony, he threw the lever that opened the trap-door and Bury fell to oblivion.

A black flag was immediately hoisted over the prison gates to inform the several thousand-strong crowd who waited outside that the sentence had been carried out. The body was allowed to hang at the end of the rope for almost an hour before being hauled back onto the scaffold. It was then placed in a roughly assembled box that served as a coffin and buried in quicklime within the prison grounds. The grave was not given a marker.

Rev. Gough made a statement to waiting news reporters as he left the prison later that morning. He said that Bury had left a written confession to his crime in which he admitted killing his wife then mutilating her body. He never gave any reasons as to why he did it.

Did the Dundee authorities capture and execute *the* 'Jack the Ripper' or did they simply deal with a copy-cat killer? The reasons for believing Bury to be the 'Whitechapel Murderer', as the Ripper was referred to at first, are numerous but largely circumstantial.

Bury was resident in London throughout the widely accepted period of the Ripper murders. He was living in Bow, which borders Whitechapel, the locus for each murder. With his employment as a sand and sawdust vendor, he would know all the thoroughfares and alleys of Whitechapel as well as anyone.

As to Bury blurting out to Lieutenant Parr 'I'm Jack the Ripper' or 'I'm *a* Jack the Ripper', the two statements have totally different meanings. Parr failed to write down either remark at the time and could only ever refer to them verbally. Perhaps he did not record them in his official notebook because he was unsure as to what the excitable little Englishman had really said to him within seconds of meeting him for the first time.

Similarly with the two scrawled chalk messages found by Lieutenant Lamb at the rear of the murder scene. At this time, two months after the last Ripper murder in London, and with the population waiting for news of him striking again soon, this type of graffiti was all too common in every city, town and village all over the country. It had even spread to some places in Europe and can, with hindsight, be considered now as the Victorian equivalent of today's 'Kilroy was here'.

The authorities placed so little value on these alleged verbal statements and scrawled messages, that no mention of either was made during Bury's trial.

Bury was known to disappear for days at a time, ostensibly while on marathon drinking sessions. In that respect, a number of theories also suggest that the Ripper would absent himself from his normal places after each murder, lying low in lodgings nearby, cleaning himself and hoping to avoid the police presence which grew in size after each subsequent killing.

There is no doubt that Bury was a very violent man and that he mutilated his wife's body. The Ripper must also have had a violent temper and he most certainly mutilated his victims. However, this is where any similarities end. The victims in Whitechapel had various injuries, ranging from their throats being cut to having their genitals and vital organs mutilated and on some occasions, removed.

The most likely sequence of events in the murder of Ellen Bury is that her husband stabbed her during another argument. She screamed when she was stabbed and he used the knife again, but this only made her cry out once more. In order to quieten her, he put the rope around her neck and she squealed. He then steadily choked her with the rope, which effectively stopped her from screaming again. Witness Duncan testified at the trial to hearing three screams, then silence.

What happened next is open to conjecture, but it is most likely Bury then stabbed his wife repeatedly while holding the rope around her neck tightly. By the time he had finished his frenzied attack, she had died from being strangled by the noose.

That scenario is unlike any of the Whitechapel attacks inasmuch as Bury appears to have panicked and then improvised. The Ripper never used a rope around the neck. To avoid any screams, the first thing he did in every attack was callously to cut the throat of each victim.

The failure of the Metropolitan Police to send someone to interview Bury after his arrest and quiz him about any possible involvement in Whitechapel at first seems to be grossly negligent. Yet it can also suggest that they thought this was unnecessary. Could that be because they already knew who the Ripper was and maybe even where he was?

However, that suggestion has to be tempered with the information that Scotland Yard's archives show that the files on the Ripper were not finally closed until 1892. The reasons for this could be that in July 1889 and February 1891, two murders occurred in Whitechapel which bore all the hallmarks of the Ripper's work.

In the former case, the pathologist, Dr Thomas Bond, whose unfortunate job had included examining most of the other Ripper victims, stated, 'I see in this murder evidence of similar design to the former Whitechapel Murders... I am of the opinion that the murder was performed by the same person who committed the former series of Whitechapel Murders'.

If the above statement of an eminent 'expert' on the style and methods of the Whitechapel Murderer is true, then it follows that Bury was not Jack the Ripper, for by the time of the first of these murders in 1889, he had been dead for two months!

The final conclusion has to be that Bury was not Jack the Ripper. He was nothing more than a drink-sodden, violent bully who stabbed and strangled his poor wife and even when the time came for him to pay the final penalty for his crime, he still did not have the decency to admit his guilt. It is now time to remove Bury's name from the official list of Ripper suspects. He does not deserve any notoriety.

The only mystery that remains in this tragedy is one that can never be answered satisfactorily. Why did the Burys choose to come to Dundee?

Footnote: William Henry Bury was the last person to be hanged in Dundee.

Four

THE ARDLAMONT MYSTERY

Scotland's judicial system has long been admired and copied all over the world. One facet of the law that is unique to this country, and which provokes much debate, is the verdict of 'Not Proven'. Of this it may suffice to say that, thanks to it being considered by many to be an unsatisfactory outcome, it has never been adopted by other nations.

In one particular case where this verdict was brought in, it provoked much public outcry and furious debate, but even so, the mystery that started it all has never been solved.

In 1890, Dudley Hambrough, a retired Army major, had, on the death of his father, inherited an estate and other properties, giving him a then substantial yearly income of around £5,000. Unfortunately, he still managed to get himself into some financial difficulty.

In order to extract himself from his money problems, the Major, as he persisted in calling himself, consulted a London financial advisor by the name of Mr Beresford Tottenham. During the course of the many meetings the two men had, the Major let it be known that, amongst other things, he was looking for ways of continuing his son Cecil's education.

The Major had decided that Cecil should follow in his footsteps and have a career in the Army. However, as his son was only 17 years old at this time, he was still too young to join up. Tottenham introduced the Major to an associate of his, Alfred John Monson. After meeting him, the Major agreed that Monson could take on the responsibility for his son's future education and well-being at an annual cost of £300, a sum the Major could only just afford.

Later that year, young Cecil went to live with Monson and his wife and children, who were, at this time, living at Ripley in Yorkshire. Cecil joined up with the local county Militia, which was a forerunner to a commission in the regular Army.

All went well for a time, and Monson even became involved in trying to help the Major with his finances. At one point, Major Hambrough had a falling out with Monson over the latter's failure to clear up the financial difficulties which still prevailed. The Major made a plea to Cecil to return to the family home, but the teenager refused, with the somewhat discourteous reply that he now considered Monson and his family to be his own.

In August 1892, Monson was declared bankrupt, owing £56,000, which made a mockery of the idea of him trying to help others with their money problems, and he and his family became totally dependent on the charity of Tottenham. Of course, this state of affairs could not continue indefinitely, and in May 1893, Monson negotiated to obtain the lease on the Scottish estate of Ardlamont in Argyllshire. Situated on a remote peninsula, the estate, comprising about 15,000 acres with shooting and fishing facilities, could only be reached by steamer from Glasgow.

As Monson was a bankrupt and could not legally conduct any business transactions, the lease was signed by Cecil and a Mr Adolphus Jerningham, who was somewhat strangely described on the lease as the young man's legal guardian. Jerningham stood guarantor for the cost of estate rental, which was £450 for the season, and fortunately was payable by instalments.

This appears to have been more of a business venture than a holiday. The idea was that Monson and Cecil would play host to guests, who would be using the estate for fishing and hunting. The annual grouse shooting season lasted only about nine weeks from its beginning in August. Thereafter the guests would be paying for the privilege of having the estate to roam in and being looked after by the Monson family and assorted servants, whose wages were being paid for by the estate owners and were included in the overall costs.

Monson, along with his wife and three children and a governess, took up residence at Ardlamont House just after the start of June. Cecil, by now 20 years of age and having been promoted to the rank of Lieutenant in the Militia the previous February, arrived a few days later, aboard the steam yacht the *Alert*. The yacht was owned by a Mr Donald, a Paisley shipbuilder, but Monson had entered into an agreement to

Alfred John Monson

purchase it for £1,200, provided he could first have the loan of it, on the pretence of having it checked over.

Cecil and Monson, playing the role of lairds to the full, were constantly in each other's company as they explored the estate. Both were interested in the outdoor life and took part in everything that was on offer.

From the outside, it appeared that Cecil was well-to-do, but in reality, both he and Monson had been making various attempts to

41

borrow money on the strength of the younger man's future inheritance, thought to be in the region of £250,000 and which he would collect on reaching 21. However every plan they tried failed.

Cecil then decided that he would take out life insurance on himself, but at first, no company would cover him. The Scottish Provident Institution in Edinburgh and the Liverpool, London and Globe Insurance Company turned down proposals for £50,000 of cover when it was revealed that the beneficiary of the policy would be Mrs Monson, who could show no legitimate interest in Cecil's life. Eventually, on 4th August 1893, the Mutual Life Assurance Company Ltd., which had offices in both New York and Glasgow, agreed.

It was at the Glasgow office that Cecil signed the forms, giving him two policies of £10,000 each. Monson, who was with Cecil, paid the first month's premium, which was £194.

Three days later, on 7th August, Cecil wrote two letters. One was sent to Mutual Life, the other to Mrs Monson. In each he assigned both policies to Mrs Monson, who would collect the monies in the event of his death.

On the 8th August, another man joined Cecil and Monson. His name was given as Edward Scott, and it was said he was an engineer and a friend of Monson. Scott had allegedly been summoned to Ardlamont to check on the engines of the yacht that was in the process of being purchased by Monson.

The circumstances of Scott's arrival at Ardlamont were strange in themselves. He was on the steamer from Glasgow, as was Monson, but they never spoke with each other at all during the trip. Monson disembarked at Kames Pier while Scott left the boat at the next stop at Tighnabruaich. Monson, having picked up his horse and trap, drove back to meet Scott and convey him to Ardlamont.

The following evening, 9th August, all three men went on a fishing trip to the nearby Ardlamont Bay. Cecil and Monson set off in a rowing boat, leaving Scott on the shore, and this is the point where the first mystery arises. The little boat sank and both men ended up in the water. Unfortunately, Cecil could not swim. Instead, he clung onto the partially submerged boat while Monson swam to the shore, got another one and rowed out to Cecil and pulled him on board.

It was after 1 a.m. before all three men arrived back at the house. Cecil and Monson were soaking wet but in high spirits. The servants, who had been wakened by the commotion, made them hot drinks and got them some dry clothing. The men sat up the rest of the night, reliving Cecil's close call with death.

The mysterious 'Edward Scott', who, in reality, was Edward Sweeney, a bookie's runner

Later that same morning, Mrs Monson, her children and the governess, were taken by Monson to the pier at Kames, about five miles from the estate, to catch the ferry for Glasgow where they were to spend the day shopping. On his return to the estate about 6 a.m., all three men then set off from the house to go rabbit hunting. Cecil was carrying a 20-bore shotgun and Monson a 12-bore. Scott was unarmed.

On that fine summer morning, they had been walking for about an hour when they reached a wood, which was still part of the estate. All three men were observed entering the wood at this time by a local resident, James Dunn, and he watched them until they disappeared from his view. What happened next in the woods has long been the subject of debate. The only thing that is absolutely certain is that Cecil was shot in the head and died almost immediately.

43

Both Monson and Scott later stated that on entering the wood, they separated from Cecil by agreement, and, a short time later, heard a shot ringing out. On calling to Cecil, they got no reply and so began a search for him. They found him soon enough, lying face down in a ditch, and when they turned him over found that he was dead.

Both men returned to Ardlamont House and alerted the staff. Two of the them, along with Monson and Scott, returned to the scene and carried Cecil's body to the house, where it was laid out on the kitchen table. A doctor was summoned, but did not attend until two hours after the event. In the interval, Monson and Scott cleaned and polished both shotguns and replaced them in the gun cupboard.

When the doctor eventually arrived, he examined the body and listened to the explanations provided by Monson and Scott. He decided that there were no suspicious circumstances and issued two death certificates, one for the authorities and the other for insurance purposes.

It would appear, in light of the information provided, that Cecil had climbed a fence, tripped or stumbled getting over it and his gun went off, fatally injuring him. All the evidence pointed to it being an unfortunate shooting accident. The Procurator Fiscal's Office at Inveraray was notified of the accident, only because the laid-down procedure specified that it needed to be done. The local police attended and completed a report on the incident.

At 5 a.m. on the morning following the shooting, Edward Scott was seen standing on the pier at Kames, awaiting the arrival of the regular steamer on its journey from Inveraray to Glasgow. The village policeman, Constable McCalman, doing his morning patrol, spoke with Scott and passed the time of day with him until the steamer's arrival.

Cecil's heartbroken father made arrangements for his son's body to be removed from the estate and taken to the Isle of Wight, the location of the family home, where Cecil's body was laid to rest in the small cemetery at Ventnor.

The matter would have ended there, were it not for one thing. About a week after Cecil's death, the Mutual Life Assurance Company was approached by Mr Tottenham, allegedly acting on the behalf of Mrs Monson, who made a claim against the recently taken out policy. This set alarm bells ringing in the company and they sent investigators to find out the facts behind the apparent accident.

On 23rd August, two insurance officials called at Ardlamont and spoke with Monson about the claim. Monson, in turn, took the men to see the Procurator Fiscal at Inveraray. What exactly was said at this meeting behind the closed doors of the office, from which Monson was excluded, is not known, although it is not too difficult to imagine. However, as soon as it was finished, a full police investigation into Cecil's death began.

The police were most interested to discover that Cecil's life insurance policy had begun less than a week before his untimely death, a fact they had been unaware of up to then. As each day passed, the investigation took unexpected turns, every one of them leading to the conclusion that foul play was involved.

The locus of the shooting had been searched again and again for clues, each time more thoroughly than the last, and what was eventually unearthed turned out to be one of the most important pieces of evidence.

About six yards from where the feet of Cecil's body lay when he fell, stood three small trees. Closer examination of the trunks of the trees revealed that each had areas where the bark had been torn away. It was assumed that the missing bark had been ripped off by a shotgun blast, although not one lead pellet was found embedded in the wood. However, the most significant part of the evidence was that the damage to the trees was about six feet above ground level, which was exactly the same height as Cecil.

While all this was going on, Monson was placed under 24-hour surveillance by two plain-clothes police officers. After losing Scott, the police were taking no chances with Monson, but as the investigation was far from completed, the officers were in plain clothes so that they could blend in with the parties of hunters that had now converged on Ardlamont House in time for the annual 'Glorious Twelfth' grouse shoot, which was well under way.

Dr McMillan, the doctor who had been first called to examine Cecil's body, was informed of the new evidence gathered in the wood, after which he withdrew the death certificates he had previously issued. This meant that the authorities could re-examine the corpse and an exhumation order was sought and granted.

Within days, Cecil's coffin was removed from its resting place and taken to a local mortuary. In law, the body could only be examined by English pathologists, but a number of Scottish-based ones were also present who visually examined the body and conferred with their English colleagues. Their findings and opinions shocked the nation.

The pathologists found that there were no powder burns or scorch marks on the body, suggesting that the fatal shot had been fired from a reasonable distance. As Cecil's right ear was missing, it was presumed that this had been totally obliterated by the blast as it was never found at all. They also collectively agreed that Cecil had been shot with a 12-bore shotgun and not his own 20-bore as thought at the time. However, they may have been assisted in coming to that conclusion when informed that the police search had recovered wadding from a 12-bore cartridge at the scene of the shooting.

The only injuries to Cecil's body were at the rear of his skull, on the right-hand side, where just four pellets had entered the skull, penetrating the brain. This had been enough to kill him. The other 160 pellets from the shotgun shell were never found. No matter which way they looked at it, the group of doctors present could find no way that these injuries could have occurred accidentally. They declared that Cecil had been murdered.

The police now believed that the fatal shot had been fired while the shotgun was being held in a horizontal position and not, as previously stated, that Cecil had fallen on top of it after tripping over. Of the large majority of pellets that had narrowly missed Cecil's head, some had torn away his ear while the others continued on past to rip the bark off the nearby trees.

Armed with all this new information, Chief Constable Fraser of the Argyll Constabulary was making his way from his headquarters in Inveraray early on the morning of 29th August 1893 to Ardlamont House, when he chanced upon Monson driving a pony and trap just outside Tighnabruaich. Aboard was a guest, who was being driven to the pier at Kames to catch a ferry, and one of the plain clothes police officers. Fraser stopped and spoke with Monson, informed him of the new circumstances and placed him under arrest for the murder, and attempted murder, of Cecil Hambrough.

Monson was taken to Tighnabruaich to await the arrival of the ferry. However, as it was still early morning and the steamer was not due until later, the three men called at the town's Royal Hotel and ate breakfast together.

Arriving later that morning at Inveraray, Monson was immediately taken to the town jail and placed in a cell. At one point during the day, he appeared before the local sheriff and was formally charged with murder and attempted murder. This latter charge stemmed from the incident the night previous to Cecil's death, when the boat had sunk. Monson failed to respond verbally to the first charge, but said in answer to the second, 'Far from attempting to murder him, I saved his life'.

MURDER

WANTED,

On a Sheriff's warrant, for being concerned in the Alleged Murder of WINDSOR DUDLEY CECIL HAMBROUGH, at Ardlamont, Argyllshire, on the 10th August, 1893,

EDWARD SWEENEY

Alias EDWARD DAVIS, alias EDWARD SCOTT,

Known in Racing Circles as

"TED DAVIS" or "LONG TED."

DESCRIPTION.

Age about 50, height about 5 feet 10 inches, thin build, broad shoulders; complexion pale, inclined to be sallow ; eyes, full, steel grey, high cheek bones, long thin face, sharp chin, dark wavy hair, brown moustache (may be shaven off); carries his shoulders well back, head slightly forward, suffers from asthma, has a habit of putting his right hand to his side when coughing, is delicate health, dresses well, and generally wears a low hard felt hat.

Is a Bookmaker or Bookmaker's Clerk, and recently resided in Sutherland Street, Pimlico, London

Information to JAMES FRASER, Chief Constable, Lochgilphead, Argyllshire, Scotland, or at any Police Station.

(Signed) **JAMES FRASER,**
Chief Constable,
Lochgilphead.

Constabulary Office,
Lochgilphead,
November 6th, 1893.

The wanted poster issued by the Argyllshire police. If brought very little response from the public.

With the arrest of Monson, all police forces in the United Kingdom received a message stating that there was now an arrest warrant in force for Scott, and if he was seen, he was to be detained. In Glasgow, the police checked all hotels and lodging houses and amazingly, at the Central Hotel in Gordon Street, found an entry dated 11th August for a Mr E. Scott and a Miss Scott. This was the same date that Scott had left Ardlamont. This couple stayed the night, in the same room, paid the bill in the morning and left. No trace of them could be found. If this was the man the police were hunting, then who was his travelling companion?

All harbours and ports were checked, in the hope that Scott may have tried to get passage from the country on a vessel, acting as an engineer. After weeks had passed, with no sightings of him at all, it was pointed out that the authorities ought to consider the possibility that the man they were so desperately seeking might, after all, not be called Edward Scott.

Could it be that this was a false name? It most certainly was, as finally the police found out that Edward Scott's real name was Edward Sweeney, and on occasions, he used the alias 'Edward Davis'. Sweeney was a London bookmaker's clerk who was better known by the nickname 'Long Ted'. Wanted posters issued by the Argyllshire Constabulary had no effect in tracing him. Later, when a £200 reward was offered, still no information on his whereabouts came to the notice of the police. It was almost as if he had vanished off the face of the earth.

Monson was kept in the jail at Inveraray for a full week. He was asked a number of times about Scott and where he could be found but during all his time there, he never uttered one word to the authorities, on the advice of his solicitor.

As an untried prisoner, Monson was entitled to wear his own clothes, have food brought in, which he did have from a local hotel, and unlimited visitors. His wife spent every day in his cell. On one occasion, Monson requested that his wife be allowed to remain in the cell overnight, but not surprisingly, this was refused. At the end of the week, he was transferred, by ferry, to Greenock Prison to await trial. He did not have long to wait.

The trial of Alfred John Monson began at Edinburgh High Court of Justiciary on 12th December 1893 and lasted for 10 days. The evidence against him was purely circumstantial, and as such, dependant upon the evidence of the many eminent expert witnesses on either side. A total of ninety-four witnesses were cited to give testimony in the case.

The three small trees were produced and passed around the court for inspection. Yet, one story about them was never told to the jury. When the trees were discovered, the police pitched a tent beside them so that the police guard had some shelter from the elements.

That night, the constable on duty disturbed a lone figure in the woods who was trying to uproot the evidence. No one was ever identified as being the culprit, although there were a few suspects.

The motive for the crimes, put forward by the prosecution, was simply that the murder was committed for monetary gain. Unfortunately for the Crown's case, their own witnesses disagreed with each other on some important points, mainly about how far and at what distance shotgun pellets begin to spread out after being fired.

In reality, these failings could have been overcome, but what hampered the prosecution most was their inability to locate Scott and bring him before the court. Although Scott was charged with the same crimes as Monson, it was thought that if he could be brought to trial, he would make a statement which would incriminate his co-accused in return for a lighter sentence.

Monson, giving evidence on his own behalf, handled all questions put to him with an air of confidence which he had maintained throughout the trial. He neatly explained that Cecil and he had exchanged shotguns shortly after leaving the house, and that is how Cecil came to be struck by the fatal discharge from the 12-bore gun.

He also strongly put across the point that he and his family depended heavily on the income provided in giving Cecil a home and education and that it would be foolhardy of him to put that income in jeopardy by killing the source.

It was a concise and logical point but whether or not that argument had any influence on the jury is debatable. More likely the jury would have thought that collecting £20,000 insurance money would be ample compensation for the loss. Even so, the glaring holes in the prosecution case could not be ignored and that led to the jury returning a unanimous verdict of 'Not Proven' after deliberating for only an hour and a quarter.

Monson was a free man. He joined up with his family and returned to spend a holiday in England. However, he had enjoyed the fame that had attached itself to him during his trial and saw it as a way of making his fortune. Monson posed for the sculpting of a waxwork model, then sued Tussaud's for putting it on display. He also made a complaint against his friend Tottenham, which resulted in his old benefactor being sentenced to three months in jail for theft.

Can the mystery of Cecil's death now be solved? First of all, with the weight of all the forensic and scientific evidence, there is no doubt that Cecil was murdered. The mystery is who committed it and why? By looking closely at the facts of the case, it might just be possible to determine both, succeeding where the trial jury failed.

Cecil decided to take out life insurance, but it could not possibly have been his own idea. Is it credible that a 20-year old was thinking about dying and even more about leaving some insurance money behind? He had £250,000 coming to him within a matter of months and if he had wanted to provide for the Monson family in the event of an early death after inheriting the money, he could have made a will, which would have been easier and cheaper!

As both Cecil and Monson were pleading poverty, the question of where the £194 for the first month's premium came from needs answering. It is a straight choice between Tottenham and Jerningham, who are both listed as 'financiers'. In reality, this was only a polite Victorian term for money lenders. Both had been spending money on Monson, and therefore indirectly on Cecil, with little to show for it, and this was a chance for either to get a return on that expenditure—with interest.

The strange matter of Cecil assigning the policies to Mrs Monson also requires comment. A popular explanation for this action was that Cecil and Mrs Monson were having an affair, and this was Cecil's way of showing just how much he loved the older woman. The most likely reason for the assigning of the policies to Mrs Monson was that, as Monson himself was a bankrupt, if he had collected any insurance pay-out, the money would have been seized and used to pay off his creditors. This could not happen if his wife came into money, from whatever source.

There is no doubt that this was the final money-making idea of Alfred John Monson and that Cecil, a young immature boy, not unlike a puppy dog, followed his master blindly. Cecil assigned the policies as he was directed. In hindsight, he was also signing his own death warrant.

The evidence points to both Monson and Scott being involved in the plot to kill Cecil, not because Monson had found out about the alleged affair and become jealous but purely for the insurance money. Tottenham was also involved, to an extent which will never be known, although he admitted in court that he was to receive £4,000 as his share of the pay-out.

However, not one of them realised that there could be no pay day as Cecil, being under 21, could not make a valid assignment of the insurance policies without the consent of his legal guardian. In this case, Jerningham should also have signed both letters of assignment. The fact that he did not turned them into worthless pieces of paper, and must have left them all dumbfounded at their basic error. Yet as far as Monson was concerned, it may have been this mistake that caused the trial jury's indecision and gave him back his freedom.

Who fired the fatal shot? In all probability it was Monson. He had hatched the plan, and over the three years he had been staying with his family, Monson had grown to dislike Cecil. Even so, he could not bring himself to do it alone and called on his friend Scott to help him, presumably for a percentage of the money.

They first tried to drown him with the set-up boating accident. The basis of the attempted murder charge was that a hole had been deliberately punched in the hull of the boat and then covered over with fishing nets, and not, as Monson said, that the sinking was caused by hitting some rocks. Experts gave evidence that, even at low tide, there were no rocks in Ardlamont Bay!

After all, if Monson had to swim back to shore and get another boat, then where was Scott? More likely than not, both were watching from the shore, hoping that Cecil would slip quietly below the surface and drown. When he continued to shout for help, Monson was forced to rescue him.

There is also the question of what happened to Scott in the months after his disappearance. The year following Monson's trial, in April 1894, Scott unexpectedly turned up at a London publishing firm. This re-appearance was prompted by the publication of a book, written by Monson and entitled *The Ardlamont Mystery Solved*. The book, or to be more precise, booklet at 72 pages long and costing a shilling, revealed nothing that had not been debated in court. Monson's only new suggestion was that Scott had been present every day in the court during the ten day trial, but no one recognised him as he was heavily disguised.

In failing to turn up at the trial, Scott had been branded an outlaw, meaning that he could be arrested at any time. Whilst in the public eye once more, thanks to his approaching the publisher, he petitioned the High Court in Edinburgh to remove this sentence that hung over him, and after a short hearing on 21st May 1894, this was done.

The reasons for this being agreed to were simple enough. Monson could not be tried twice for the same crime, and if the authorities could not convict him with the evidence they had, then they certainly would not be able to secure a conviction against Scott. The Crown even failed to send a representative to the hearing, such was their lack of interest.

In April 1895, Monson also turned up in Edinburgh as part of a hypnotist's show being staged at the city's Operetta House. The idea was that Monson would be put into a trance and then answer questions from the audience on the mystery. However, by this date, his notoriety was waning considerably and after only a handful of performances, during which he consistently failed to answer the more probing questions put to him, Monson was released from his contract.

Monson was now free to return to doing what he did best—working on schemes to cheat insurance companies. In 1898 he was found guilty of attempting to defraud the Norwich Union Life Assurance Company and sentenced to 5 years imprisonment.

While in jail, Monson decided to divorce his wife. His grounds were stated to be that: 'Mrs Monson was guilty of infidelity in 1891 with a person unknown and again later the same year with another person. The other person is the late Cecil Hambrough'. Could this have been the real reason for the murder of the young man? Or did Monson, in true hunting fashion, kill two problems with one shot?

After serving his full sentence, Monson was released in 1903. He tasted only a few months of liberty before he died, aged 43 years. He passed away with no family or friends present and as he had spent most of his life—penniless. Very soon, the public forgot all about the Ardlamont affair, but the mystery of who really killed Cecil Hambrough—and why—remained.

One further sad irony of the case, not connected to any of the participants, occurred during the course of the trial. Amid all the publicity that the case attracted, Henry Cord, a gamekeeper on an estate at Walhampton in England, was attempting to show a group of fellow workers how it was possible that Cecil had shot himself. In demonstrating his version of events, Cord accidentally shot and killed himself, leaving a widow and five children.

Five

THE DESERTED BEACON

In most incidents involving elements of mystery, myths build up around the facts of the case, attaching themselves so well over a period of time, that it is sometimes difficult to separate them from the real facts at a later date to get at the truth. This mystery is no different.

Just over 20 miles to the north-west of Gallan Head on the Isle of Lewis, out in the grey waters of the North Atlantic, sit seven small islands collectively called The Flannen Isles. The largest of the islands, unimaginatively named Eilean Mor (Big Island), whose cliffs rise sheer from the sea to almost 200 feet, measures only 500 yards in length by 200 yards at its widest point.

The islands are also known by the name 'The Seven Hunters' and perhaps this title is more appropriate, for like a hunter patiently lying in wait for its prey, so these islands wait at the end of a vast stretch of open ocean, occasionally hidden from view by the large swells of the sea that roll towards them unhindered for almost 3,000 miles. The island's jagged rocks and raging surf have snared and wrecked many vessels whose journeys took them too close to their perilous shores.

In the latter half of the nineteenth century, the amount of sea-going traffic increased dramatically and the Flannen Isles lay directly on the route that vessels arriving from North America would steer while aiming for passage around the Pentland Firth and east coast ports. After much outcry over the unacceptable number of shipwrecks, a decision was taken to build a lighthouse on the islands and the firm of David and Charles Stevenson successfully tendered for and undertook the task. Although they were experienced lighthouse builders, this was their most difficult job to date. In 1895, at the start of construction, the isles were considered to be the world's most isolated location for a lighthouse.

The site selected was on Eilean Mor, and the first difficulty arose in just trying to get workers ashore. Two landing areas were eventually dynamited out of the rocks, one on the west side of the island, the other on the east side. As both these piers were at sea level, the next difficulty to overcome was that of getting up and over the sheer cliffs. Again, dynamite was used to blast two herring-bone stairways leading upwards and eventually onto the grassy plateau on the top of the island.

About halfway up the cliff face, concrete platforms were put in place and on each was bolted a crane for lifting all the building materials, which had to be transported by ship to the islands, up and onto a small railway that had been built to run from the clifftop to the lighthouse buildings.

Because of the island's extremely hard gneiss rocks and the inhospitable weather, which had necessitated the lighthouse in the first place, building progressed very slowly, and it was not until fully four years after work first began that the lantern in the 75-foot white-painted tower was lit for the first time.

On 7th December 1899, the Flannen Isles lighthouse began operations. Sited on the highest point of the island, it stood 330 feet above the ocean, and its 140,000 candle-power lamp could be seen for at least 25 miles distant. On certain nights of clear weather, it was reckoned that its two flashes every half a minute could be seen almost 40 miles away.

The lighthouse was manned by a team of four keepers working a rota system whereby they spent six weeks on the island with two weeks leave on shore at home. This meant that there were only ever three keepers on duty at any one time.

The Principal Keeper was 43-year-old James Ducat, a native of Arbroath and a married man with four children. He had been in the service of the Northern Lighthouse Board (N.L.B.) for 21 years and was considered to be one of their most experienced and reliable men. The three Assistant Keepers were William Ross, Joseph Moore and Thomas Marshall. Marshall was the only single man in the group. All had been hand-picked by Superintendent Robert Muirhead of the N.L.B., who considered it imperative to get the right men in place when setting up a new lighthouse station.

All went well over the months of the first winter and during the summer, Muirhead spent a number of weeks with the keepers, during

The lighthouse atop Eilean Mor, Flannen Isles

which time they all worked together to put right some very minor teething problems. The cranes previously used in the construction had been left in place as they were needed to assist in the running of the lighthouse. One look at the list of supplies regularly ferried to the island confirms this. It included 1,250 gallons of water, all in wooden barrels, and 1,200 gallons of paraffin, contained in 40-gallon metal drums. In addition, several tons of coal were also required to operate the railway and for heating and cooking. There was no way any of these items could be carried up the cliff staircase by the keepers.

Around the end of November 1900, Assistant Keeper Ross became ill and returned to the mainland to recuperate. The situation of being a man short had been foreseen and catered for and Occasional Keeper Donald McArthur, a 40-year-old married man from Lewis, was brought in to cover for the sick man.

On 7th December 1900 the lighthouse tender *Hesperus* paid its usual call to the lighthouse to deliver the regular supplies to the Keepers. Also on board was Superintendant Muirhead and McArthur, who was to relieve Joseph Moore, the next in line for shore leave. Moore was scheduled to return two weeks later to replace Marshall, who was the only one of the four rostered to spend Christmas and New Year at home.

About midnight on 15 December, the lookout aboard the SS *Archtor*, en route from Philadelphia to Leith, was scanning the night horizons, no doubt dreaming of spending the upcoming holidays with his loved ones. Although the sea had a fair swell on it, the night was fine and he could clearly identify the outlines of the Flannen Isles about 6 miles away. What he could not see was the blinking of its warning beacon.

On being informed of this, Captain Holman raised his telescope and focused on the island. All he saw through his lens was the darkened silhouette of the lighthouse. On reaching port on 18 December, he reported the matter to his employers, agents for Cosmopolitan Line Steamers, but unbelievably, the information was never relayed to the N.L.B. due to a breakdown in communications, or, as it was put at the time, 'because other more pressing matters caused it to escape from memory'.

Violent storms had been raging throughout Scotland, almost one after the other, since just before the middle of December. As a result, the planned relief of the Flannen lighthouse for 20 December could not take place and it was not until Boxing Day, when the weather moderated sufficiently, that the *Hesperus* could sail from East Loch Roag on Lewis with supplies and the Relief Keeper Moore.

About midday, the *Hesperus* reached Eilean Mor. Captain James Harvie had decided to approach the east landing, as it was the more sheltered side of the island. As the vessel neared, those on board noticed immediately that something was amiss. There was no welcoming flag hoisted on the lighthouse pole. Not too much was read into this however, as it was possible the keepers were busy at work out of sight of the east side of the island, and therefore they had not noticed the ship approaching.

Harvie ordered the ship's whistle to be sounded, but the shrill blast brought only thousands of sea birds from their perches on the cliff face, noisy and angry at being so rudely disturbed. There was no movement in or around the buildings of the lighthouse. With mounting astonishment, Harvey ordered a rocket to be fired over the island, and although it burst its colourful contents with a loud explosion, still nothing was seen of the keepers.

Moore was instructed to go ashore and find out what the problem was. Thoughts that the keepers were ill and could not venture out of the lighthouse seemed to be the most reasonable explanation for their non-appearance, as Moore climbed aboard the small tender and was rowed ashore. With some initial difficulty, he eventually landed and began making his way up the steep stone staircase towards the beacon.

On reaching the top of the cliffs, Moore began running along the pathway towards the tower. The entrance gate of the yard, within which all the buildings stood, was closed. Opening it, he moved towards the lighthouse itself. The front door was closed but not locked. He opened that and moved inside, only to be confronted by another closed door. As he moved through it, Moore found the kitchen door now facing him was wide open and cautiously he entered. Ever since he arrived at the building, he had been calling out the names of his colleagues, but no one answered his shouts.

Once in the kitchen, he immediately noticed that two chairs were standing next to the table, but that the third chair had been knocked over and was lying on its side. In the fireplace lay cold ashes and the clock on the shelf above had stopped running. All the pots and pans were clean and stacked neatly in their usual places. He then went to the bedrooms and found that the beds were unmade, just as they would be after someone had risen from them.

By now, Moore was finding it difficult to contain his feelings. The hairs on the back of his neck were standing to attention, and deciding that enough was enough, he took fright, turned and fled the lighthouse, running all the way back to the landing point. He breathlessly explained to the crew of the small boat what he had found and two of the men volunteered to go back up to the lighthouse with him to search more thoroughly.

This group of three combed the outbuildings and the lighthouse itself. On reaching the top of the tower, they found that the wicks in the lamp had been cleaned and trimmed, ready for use, and the paraffin oil reservoirs were full. The blinds had been drawn, which the keepers were required to do during daylight hours. The shades were to prevent the sun being magnified by the powerful lens of the lighthouse and then possibly setting off a fire. The only two things not normal here were that the protective cover was not in place over the lantern and a thin film of dust was present on the lens itself.

In the Duty Room, Moore found the Keepers Log, which had last been written up on 13 December, almost two weeks before. Above the writing desk, where the log was maintained, hung a large slate. On it were two entries, written in chalk, one for the 14th and the other for the 15th.

This was the normal practice. Entries to be entered in the log, which was kept by Ducat, would first be written on the slate, for transfer later to the permanent record book. The entry for the 14th showed the time of lighting the beacon, while the entry for the 15th detailed when the light was extinguished and the weather and barometer readings taken that morning at 9 a.m. The information was that it was raining incessantly.

When the search was completed, there was still no trace of the three keepers. Rather than begin a full scale search of the entire island at this time, the men returned to the east landing and rowed back to the *Hesperus*, where they informed Harvey what they had found— and what they had not!

The Captain instructed that Moore should return to the island and man the lighthouse. Three men from the tender, MacDonald, the Buoymaster, and seamen Lamont and Campbell volunteered to assist in these duties. Once they were safely ashore, the *Hesperus* sailed for the lighthouse shore station at Breasclete on Lewis, from where Harvie sent an urgent telegram to the N.L.B. Headquarters in George Street, Edinburgh. The telegram read:

A dreadful accident has happened at Flannens. The three Keepers, Ducat, Marshall and the Occasional have disappeared from the Island. On our arrival there this afternoon no signs of life were to be seen on the Island. Fired a rocket, but, as no response was made, managed to land Moore, who went up to the station but found no Keepers there. The clocks were stopped and other signs indicated that the accident must have happened about a week ago. Poor fellows must have been blown over the cliffs or drowned trying to secure a crane or something like that. Night coming on, we could not wait to make further investigation, but will go off again tomorrow morning to try and learn something as to their fate. I have left Moore, MacDonald, Buoymaster and two seamen on the Island to keep the light burning until you make other arrangements. Will not return to Oban until I hear from you. I have repeated this wire to Muirhead, in case you are not at home. I will remain at the telegraph office tonight until it closes, if you wish to wire me.

Master, *Hesperus*

By now, it was well after 8 p.m. and the telegram boy tried the offices in George Street first, but because of the Christmas holidays and the time of day, they were closed. He then cycled to the home of William Murdoch, Secretary of the Board, who read the telegram repeatedly but could not believe it.

The lantern on Flannen was lit that Boxing Day afternoon and Moore sat up through the night, filling the paraffin reservoirs regularly. The following morning, after extinguishing the lamp and having breakfast, the men then began a detailed search of the island itself. Every nook and cranny was sought out and searched thoroughly, but still nothing relating to the three keepers was found. It was not until the searchers arrived at the west landing area that some understanding of what might have happened to the keepers began to emerge.

For about 30 feet along the top edge of the cliff, the grassy turf had been torn away. On climbing down the staircase to the derrick holding the crane, which was about 80 feet above sea level, the men discovered that a large number of the railings around the platform were broken away. A box, which was used to store ropes and crane handles and was always secreted in a rock crevice a further thirty feet above the crane, was also gone, but some of the ropes, still securely coiled, thus evidently never used, were found lying around the crane base, as were some of the spare handles.

A lifebuoy that had been secured to the railings was missing, yet its securing straps were still attached to the railings. A large boulder, estimated at weighing over a ton and which had been a fixture on the cliff, had been moved a great distance down the stairway, coming to rest on it and partially blocking it. This scene of destruction still failed to reveal a single clue as to the whereabouts of the keepers.

The men returned to the lighthouse and Moore began examining the living quarters in greater detail. In one of the cupboards he found that both Ducat and Marshall's oilskins and boots were missing from their usual places, although McArthur's waterproof clothing was still hanging on its hooks. Moore stated that the only time any of the keepers would wear these items was when going out to work at one of the landing places.

When all the searches were completed and nothing more could be done, other than to speculate on how the keepers disappeared, Moore sat down and wrote a report of the incident, in the form of a letter, detailing all he had found and his own suspicions about the mysterious circumstances. That he found this difficult to do there is no doubt, but it must also have helped him in some small way to come to terms with the finality of his three colleagues' fate. However, such was Moore's state of mind that it was later recommended that if his nerves did not improve he should be transferred.

Superintendent Muirhead arrived on Flannen on 29th December, accompanied by two relief keepers, to take over from the *Hesperus* crewmen. Muirhead then went over every detail with Moore and obviously felt deeply shocked at what had occurred. He admitted that feelings of guilt lay heavily upon him as he had selected each man personally for the posting.

When Muirhead eventually left the island later that day, he paid personal visits to Mrs Ducat and Mrs McArthur to offer his condolences. He also made enquiries with Roderick McKenzie, a gamekeeper at Uig on Lewis, who was employed by the N.L.B. to keep a diary of when he could see the Flannen light and when he could not see it and to report the same. For these observation duties, McKenzie was paid £8 per year.

Muirhead examined the Record Book and found that the last time McKenzie had noted seeing the beam from Flannen had been on the night of 12th December. McKenzie stated to the Superintendent, and this was verified by earlier entries in the diary, that the light was sometimes not seen for five or six days at a time due to the weather. However, by Christmas Eve, McKenzie, worried at not seeing anything for twelve consecutive nights, asked his neighbours to keep a special watch for the light.

Once the newspapers got hold of the story, theories about the keepers disappearance were widespread. As the mystery has never conclusively been solved, for almost a century more and more explanations as to what happened to the three keepers have been added to the list.

Some suggestions have been the work of fertile imaginations, while others have been shamefully derogatory to the memories of the three men who lost their lives. One example of the latter was a work which suggested that the missing keepers were all homosexuals and that their affair turned to violence through jealously and rejection, ending in murder and suicide.

Another theory speculates that one of the keepers was an alcoholic, or alternatively, criminally insane, that he murdered his two colleagues and afterwards, in a fit of remorse, threw himself to his death from the cliffs. While these three scenarios have a recurring theme—murder and suicide—none has a grain of truth in them. To even consider them for a moment, or comment upon them, might in some way lend a little credence to them when they truly deserve none.

One of the prime sources of so many of the myths in this particular case is a poem, written in 1912 by W. W. Gibson. In the course of this, Gibson suggests that on the kitchen table of the lighthouse when Moore entered was a meal of 'meat and cheese and bread' and that it was 'untouched'. In the re-telling of this part of the story over the years, the menu of the meal has been altered to include potatoes and pickles and sometimes bowls of soup. Moore's actual account, written two days after his arrival and detailing everything he had found, makes no mention of this 'meal' laid out on the table. In fact, Moore says specifically that the kitchen utensils were all cleaned and stacked neatly.

Occasionally, the mysterious disappearance of the three keepers has been characterised as a landlocked equivalent of the maritime *Marie Celeste* affair. Like the lighthouse, the ship was in neat and tidy order throughout when found and boarded, with no obvious reasons apparent for the abandoning of the vessel. It is said that a meal was laid out in the captain's cabin but, like the lighthouse one, it had been untouched. Perhaps this is where Gibson got the idea for use in his poem? As a small example of how facts can become distorted through the passage of time, the correct name for the vessel was the *Mary Celeste* and not as most publications would term it.

Another myth begun by Gibson's poem is that the three keepers were, by some supernatural force or other, turned into three ugly black sea-birds, the doing of which was a form of revenge for the disturbing of the island with 'modern' technology. In the sixth or seventh century, St Flann, a Christian hermit, stayed on the island and built himself a chapel that also doubled as his shelter from the elements. There are ruins of a building only a matter of yards from the lighthouse tower which can still be seen today. Whether they are the remains of St. Flann's hermitage or a much later construction has never been established.

In a similar vein was the suggestion that the island was cursed in some way or another, as in previous years, four men had drowned while trying to get ashore from the relief ship, while a previous keeper is alleged to have thrown himself from the tower while depressed. If these events had happened then it would indicate an atrocious record for a lighthouse. However, those who subscribed to this theory conveniently forgot that the lighthouse had only been in existence for one year. In reality, these events just never happened. Again, Gibson's poem perpetuates the fantasy.

Added to all this are the theories that the keepers were abducted by a UFO (obviously only suggested once UFO's themselves became the subject of debate), or that a large sea-serpent invaded the island, and finally that the three men were murdered by agents of a foreign power after they had observed a top secret experiment, perhaps involving a new type of ship. A variation on this particular theme was that the agents were British and the keepers were forcibly removed from the island to spend the rest of their natural lives in solitary confinement! This theory invites one question that has never been satisfactorily answered. What kind of super new or experimental vessel could it have been that was being tested in the storm-tossed winter waters of the North Atlantic in absolutely atrocious weather conditions?

Having discounted the more fanciful theories of what happened to the three keepers, attention can turn now to what really could have taken place and caused Ducat, Marshall and McArthur to vanish.

The most logical argument put forward and which must be given the most serious consideration, is the lengthy report written by Muirhead after his visit to the island in the aftermath of the incident. It was intended to explain the possible events to his superiors and is dated 8th January 1901. Part of his report reads:

Everything at the east landing place was in order and the ropes which had been coiled and stored there on completion of the relief on the 7th December were all in their places, and in the lighthouse buildings and at the station everything was in order. Owing to the amount of sea, I could not get down to the landing place, but I got down to the crane platform about 70 feet above the sea level. The crane originally erected on this platform was washed away during last winter, and the crane put up this summer was found to be unharmed, the jib lowered and secured to the rock, and the canvas covering the wire rope on the barrel securely lashed round it, and there was no evidence that the men had been doing anything at the crane. The mooring ropes, land-ing ropes, derrick landing ropes and crane handles, and also a wooden box in which they were kept and was secured in a crevice in the rocks about 70 feet up the tramway from its terminus, and about 40 feet higher than the crane platform, or 110 feet in all above sea level, had been washed away, and the ropes were strewn in the crevices of the rocks near the crane platform and entangled among the crane legs, but they were all coiled up, no single coil being found unfastened. The iron railings round the crane platform and from the terminus of the tramway to the concrete steps up from the west landing, were displaced and twisted. A large block of stone weighing upwards of 20 cwt, had been dislodged from its position higher up and carried down to and left on the concrete path leading from the terminus of the tram-way to the top of the steps. A lifebuoy fastened to the railings along the path, to be used in case of emergency, had disappeared, and I thought at first that it had been removed for the purpose of being used but, on examining the ropes by which it was fastened, I found that they had not been touched, and as pieces of canvas were adhering to the ropes, it was evident that the force of the sea pouring through the railings had, even at this great height (110 feet above sea level), torn the lifebuoy off the ropes.

When the accident occurred, Ducat was wearing sea boots and a waterproof, and Marshall sea boots and oilskins, and as Moore assures me that the men only wore these articles when going down to the landings, they must have intended, when they left the station, either to go down to the landing or the proximity of it. After a careful examination of the place, the railings, ropes etc. and weighing all the evidence I could secure, I am of the opinion that the most likely explanation of the disappearance of the three men is that they had all gone down on the afternoon of Saturday 15th December to the proximity of the west landing, to secure the box with the mooring ropes etc. and that an unexpectedly large roller had come up on the island, and a large body of water going up higher than where they were and coming down on them had swept them away with resistless force. I have considered and discussed the possibility of the men being blown away by the wind, but, as the wind was westerly, I am of the opinion notwithstanding its great force, that the more probable explanation is that they have been washed away as, had the wind caught them, it would from its direction, have blown them up the island and I feel certain that they would have managed to throw themselves down before they had reached the summit or brow of the island.

What Muirhead was suggesting is that after the storms which had kept the keepers indoors for a few days had abated, Ducat, Marshall and McArthur had all donned their inclement weather gear to go to the west landing to check or repair any possible damage done in that area. Yet, Muirhead seems to have forgotten that McArthur's boots and oilskins had been found in their rightful place in the lighthouse station and the fact that the rules governing the operating of the lighthouse stated that one man must be present in the lighthouse at all times.

An interesting fact not often referred to is that, although he had 21 years' service, Ducat had very little experience of island lighthouses and certainly of none in such a hostile environment. His only other similar island posting had been to Inchkeith in the relatively quiet waters of the Firth of Forth in 1884. Marshall, with less than five years service, was also lacking in island experience.

Over the years following the disappearance, a phenomenon was observed on many occasions on Flannen. This was the sudden appearance of a larger than usual wave coming out of nowhere and bearing down on the little island. These large waves, similar to tidal waves, have on occasions been reported to be as high as 300 feet. What was also noted was that the appearance of these huge waves coincided with the end of two or three days of violent stormy weather far out into the Atlantic ocean. Although Ducat was lacking experience, he should certainly have been aware of this danger on Flannen, as evidenced by the washing away of the crane the previous winter.

Could it have been that while Ducat and Marshall were busily working away at the west landing area, McArthur, as the junior man, was doing his duties as cook, and at work tidying up the living quarters, when he saw a mountainous wave bearing down on his colleagues? McArthur, with no time to don his waterproof clothing, immediately ran out of the lighthouse and down towards the west landing, accidentally knocking his chair over in his hurry.

On reaching the cliff-top, he might have had time to shout a warning, but whether it reached the ears of his colleagues below or was carried away on the wind is irrelevant, because by now it was too late. The sheer wall of water fell on the three men, at different levels, and swept them up and off the island, along with everything else that was later reported missing.

All of this occurred on Saturday 15th December, between 9 a.m. and 3.20 p.m., the times between the recording of the weather and barometer readings on the slate and the intended lighting-up time for the beacon that day. The *Archtor* reported being unable to see the light that night, so it is safe to assume that it had never been lit that day. One other point is that the keepers would not attempt to work outside in the darkness. Any work needing done could always wait until the following day during daylight.

It is possible to confine the time of the keepers' disappearance to the Saturday afternoon by careful examination of the facts. After breakfast each morning, the keepers' duties would be to clean the lantern room and fill the paraffin tanks, including the reserve containers. This work normally took all of or, at the very least, the best part of the morning. After lunch, which was always around 1 p.m, the afternoon would be spent carrying out repairs or maintenance to anything requiring it.

From the condition of the lighthouse, as found by Moore and the men from the *Hesperus*, that morning's chores realting to the beacon had been completed and lunch was not being prepared but in fact was over, as the neat and tidy kitchen suggests. This evidence points to the fact that whatever happened to the men did so in the approximately two-hour period between 1.30 p.m. and 3.20 p.m.

Unusually, the bodies of the men were never washed ashore on the Flannens or elsewhere, which helps those who wish to continue with the belief in supernatural involvement.

Probably as a consequence of Muirhead's thorough report, the

Crown Office in Edinburgh decided, in July 1901, after examining all the facts, that no purpose would be served by holding a Fatal Accident Inquiry. If no one could then come up with a cast-iron cause for the mysterious disappearance of the three keepers, can we now expect to solve it?

Since that fateful date, the Flannen Isles light has shone without further mishap. In 1971, the last keepers departed and it was switched over to full automation, the only visitors now being a once-yearly maintenance crew and the many species of sea-birds—and, if the local superstition is to be believed, the three dark spectres that can be seen on certain nights.

Six

ROBBERY OR REVENGE?

On an isolated peninsula of the Ayrshire coastline, almost halfway between Fairlie and Seamill, stands the small village of Portencross. Even today, it only numbers a handful of houses guarding a ruined castle that stands almost on the shore. In 1913, at the furthest part of the village, where the road ends, stood a whitewashed cottage called Northbank.

It was a two-storey, eight-roomed dwelling, surrounded on three sides by lovingly tended gardens, and was home to a retired couple and a younger relative. But what happened here on a stormy October night in that year changed the lives of those involved forever. The mystery of who could have comitted such a terrible act has never been solved.

The cottage was occupied by Alexander McLaren, a 60-year-old retired businessman, his wife Jessie and her sister, 49-year-old Mary Gunn. Although all three were Ayrshire people born and bred, they had not always lived at Northbank. Some twenty or so years before, when the McLarens first married, they lived in Kilmarnock, where Mr McLaren worked in the steel industry.

Having saved enough money, added to an inheritance Mrs McLaren received when her father died, the couple moved to Port William in Wigtownshire, where they owned and operated a bakery business.

As a result of the death of her father and the moving away of her sister and brother-in-law, Mary Gunn was forced, through necessity, to find employment. She gained a supervisor's position at the Beith telephone exchange and then a similar post at Ardrossan. She also earned a reputation as something of a local beauty and was known to all as 'the Beauty of Beith'. However, despite her many admirers, she never married, probably because of the fact that she had an elderly and sick mother to look after.

So successful did the McLaren's bakery business become that, within a short space of time, they were able to offer to have the elderly mother come and live with them permanently. The offer also included Mary Gunn and with it, for her, the job of managing the bakery.

The situation remained like this for several years until Mr McLaren decided he wanted to try his hand at farming. He made enquiries and was successful in leasing a dairy farm at Glenoe, just outside Taynuilt in Argyllshire. The McLarens and old Mrs Gunn moved there, leaving Mary in sole charge of the bakery.

After about two years, the bakery business was sold off and Mary Gunn joined the rest of her family at Glenoe. Unfortunately, their happiness was short-lived as her mother died soon after her arrival. With nothing to hold her and farm life not agreeing with her, Mary sailed for Canada and went to live with relatives in the province of Saskatchewan.

The McLarens were now finding life difficult on the farm. Mrs McLaren had just turned 60 and her husband was only months younger. With Mary gone, there was no one to help with the work. It did not take them too long to decide to give up and retire to live comfortably, thanks to the profits from the sale of the bakery.

The McLarens returned to the area of their birth and in May 1913, leased Northbank Cottage. Standing about 30 yards back from the shoreline, and nestling under some cliffs known locally as the Three Sisters, it seemed an idyllic spot to spend quietly their remaining days.

The McLarens wrote to Mary in Canada and again invited her to join them, this time at their new home. Mary did not need to be asked twice as she was not enjoying the life she had chosen. If anything, she found that Canadian rural life was much more harsh than that of her homeland. She sailed back to Scotland immediately and all three settled into Northbank.

The family group soon became well known and respected in the areas of Portencross and nearby West Kilbride. Mr McLaren was occasionally away on business, tying up the loose ends of the farm venture, and Mary was regularly seen out shopping for their needs.

Saturday, 18th October 1913, was like any other normal day for the occupants of Northbank, one exception. Mr McLaren had to travel to Perth that day in order to attend the cattle market there. He was settling his final piece of business in relation to the farm by selling off his livestock. He rose early and caught the train to Glasgow.

About 3 p.m., Mary Gunn left Northbank and walked to West Kilbride to do some shopping, and after some two hours, she was making her way back towards the cottage. In her absence, Mr McLaren had returned earlier than expected, his business successfully concluded. He was not long in the house when he decided to set off to meet Mary on the road and escort her home.

Having met her near to Ardneil Farm, which was about a mile from the cottage, they walked together in the direction of Northbank. About five minutes into their journey, they met and spoke with the driver of the local bus, who knew them both by sight. After exchanging pleasantries with him, they continued on their way.

Once at home, their cow was milked and they sat down to enjoy their evening meal. As they finished the meal, it was getting dark and they all went in to the sitting room where the lamps were already lit. Sitting round a roaring fire, Mr McLaren began reading aloud from a book by W.W. Jacobs as they two women listened and knitted at the same time. Although this was a nightly occurrence in the house, the scene of gentle contentment was to last for less than an hour.

Almost on the stroke of 9 p.m., with a storm gathering anger every minute, as indicated by the wind howling in the chimney, six gunshots rang out around the room in the space of ten or fifteen seconds.

The first shot exploded from the window in the far corner of the room. It failed to find its intended target, instead grazing the arm of the sitting chair that McLaren was in. It would be discovered later, embedded in the stuffing of the chair back.

Obviously startled by the thundering noise of the gunshot echoing in the room, all three immediately stood up. Two further gunshots rang out and Mary Gunn cried, 'Oh Alex, I'm shot' and fell face down onto the stone floor. Almost immediately, another two shots screamed across the room and Mrs McLaren slumped backwards into the chair she had just risen from. She managed to gasp, 'I think I'm shot too'.

McLaren, still on his feet, went to his wife's aid. He had the presence of mind to get her out of the chair and onto the floor. The room was now deafeningly quiet, but full of choking smoke from the gun. At this point, McLaren realised that he had also been shot. Two of his fingers were bleeding and there was a bullet hole through the book that he was still holding. Little torn pieces of paper from the pages fluttered slowly to the floor like confetti.

All remained quiet for the next minute or so—even the wind had dropped—and during this time McLaren regained some of his composure. He tried to rouse Mary Gunn but got no response. He did not realise it, or if he did, he said nothing to his wife, but his sister-in-law was dead. He ensured that his wife was comfortable and then ventured slowly and cautiously outside the cottage. He saw and heard no one.

His first priority was to get help for his injured wife and he made his way to Cross Farm, the nearest house to Northbank but still almost half a mile away. About ten minutes later he arrived, banging on the door, exhausted and blood from his hand now smeared over his face and clothes. The shocked neighbour took McLaren to another nearby house, which was one of the few in the district to have a telephone. From there, the police in West Kilbride were summoned to the scene.

The police arrived relatively quickly, considering the remoteness of the place. They were helped in this by a commandeered motor vehicle, as they had no transport of their own.

Mrs McLaren was made comfortable and a doctor was summoned. When he arrived, he pronounced Mary Gunn to be dead and began treating the wounds of the McLarens. Mrs McLaren was suffering from a wound to her back, the bullet having lodged in the area of her kidneys. Mr McLaren's damaged hand was stitched and bandaged.

The police inquiry continued all night long, but there was not much that they could do due to the darkness, made even blacker and more inhospitable by the now raging storm. Two further doctors were summoned and operated on Mrs McLaren during the night while she lay in her own bed. Later that week her condition worsened as infection set in and she was removed to Kilmarnock Infirmary.

The doctors also carried out an immediate post mortem examination on Mary Gunn, which revealed that she had been struck by two bullets, one of which went clean through her heart. Death had been almost instantaneous.

A minute examination of the sitting room revealed the previously mentioned bullet lodged in the backing of McLaren's chair. Two more bullets were dug out from the plasterwork of the wall above the fireplace. One was that which had torn through McLaren's fingers and the book. The other was thought to have been one of the two that had struck Mary Gunn.

Northbank Cottage. The cross marks the window through which the murderer fired the fatal shots.

The area of the corner window was examined and two panes of glass at the bottom part were found to be broken. Some splinters from the wooden window frame were also found, and it was presumed that at least one of the bullets hit the framework. A search outside revealed the sixth and final bullet lying on the ground.

When the position of the window in relation to where the victims of the shooting were sitting was taken into consideration, it was established that whoever had fired the shots had been aiming the weapon in an area where the viewpoint was an opening of only two inches wide. It was therefore not surprising to find that part of the window's frame was damaged.

Unfortunately, no fingerprint impressions were discovered on the frame. What was discovered and was to later turn out an important clue was a set of footprints outside the windows in the garden. Due to the soft sandy soil in the garden, the impressions were covered over with blankets in an effort to prevent them from deteriorating prior to moulds being obtained.

In actual fact, three sets of footprints were discovered. Two sets were easily identified, one belonging to one of the searching officers and the other thought to be those of either Mrs McLaren or Miss Gunn, presumably put there when gardening. The third set of footprints could not be identified and many theories were expounded about them. That they belonged to the murderer the police had no doubt.

However, the police were aware that footprints do not lead to a murderer. If they have a suspect, then comparisons can be made between his footwear and the impressions found. If they match, then this becomes a piece of incriminating evidence to be brought out at any future criminal proceedings.

Probably the most outrageous suggestion about the footprints was that they were similar to the marks made by golfers' shoes, and as a result, the footprints became known as the 'Golf Shoe Footprints'. Imagine the lunacy of firing six shots, killing one person and injuring another two, and then making a getaway wearing spiked shoes!

Not until the morning came, the howling wind having abated, were reinforcements brought in and areas around the cottage searched. The police were now actively hunting the culprit and his weapon.

The police were adamant that as they had arrived at the scene in the shortest time possible, and with their roadblocks also having been put in place just as quickly, they concluded that the culprit must still be in the district. The remoteness of the cottage meant that any vehicular traffic coming from that direction would have been observed, probably by the police travelling to the scene. The only conclusion to be reached therefore was that the escape had been made on foot, along the coastal path.

As the path to Seamill ran parallel to the road and therefore anyone on it would be seen, it was discounted. By elimination, it was thought most likely that the murderer had used the path towards Fairlie as his escape route. This in turn led police to believe that the murderer was a local person or someone who knew the area well.

The police search was widened and took in both the shoreline and coastal paths in the area. A local joiner was contracted and instructed to make a number of wooden boxes with glass bottoms. Armed with these, the searchers then took to numerous small rowing boats and attempted to scan the bottom of the Clyde, looking for any discarded weapon.

However, the area being searched in this manner, although close to the shore, was still quite deep and the search proved to be a complete waste of time as the bottom of the sea could not be seen. Also, with the informed view being that the culprit had made off along the coastal path towards Fairlie, this would have meant him taking a detour of considerable distance to throw the weapon into the water, then retracing his steps to regain the pathway. A dangerous thing to do when time is important and a storm raging.

Rumour had it that a small boat, normally moored near to the cottage, was missing and therefore the culprit had made his escape in this. Even before the little vessel turned up, this idea was discounted because of the violent storm at the time and the fact that the nearest place across the water was the island of Cumbrae.

Apart from the footprints in the garden, the police had also recovered the six bullets that had been fired. When examined, they were found to be of a large calibre, .45, and were thought to have been fired from an Army service revolver or old fashioned Colt-type gun.

This fact produced their first lead when they received information that ammunition of this type had recently been purchased by a man in Ardrossan. A speedy visit to his house showed that he had indeed bought a box of bullets, but of .404 calibre. He was eliminated from the inquiry.

One point that must be considered, however, is that the weapon used was an extremely powerful handgun. Added to this was the narrow angle of fire and yet, with six shots fired in rapid succession, the assailant managed to find the target on four occasions and narrowly missed once. From this, we can safely assume that the weapon was used by someone who was very proficient with firearms.

Information also came to them that a man had attempted to board a train at Largs Railway Station on the Saturday night without a ticket, and this had, in turn, led to a disturbance. The police had the story published in the local newspapers in the hope that other passengers might come forward as witnesses. Instead, a well-known local man called at the investigation headquarters to inform the police that he was the traveller they sought.

He explained that after enjoying a night out in the town, he had insufficient money for a first-class fare and had asked the ticket clerk that he be billed for it at a later date. The clerk refused and an argument developed. The passenger subsequently purchased a third-class ticket and journeyed home. He only came forward when he was horrified to read in the local press that the police were actively searching for him, as he was considered to be a suspect.

A motive for the murderous attack at Northbank was sought. Statements were made by Mr McLaren and published for all and sundry to read. He stated that he had no enemies and could only consider that the motive was robbery.

The robbery motive was widely considered to be the reason for the murderous attack, as McLaren, having returned from the cattle sale in Perth, was thought to be in possession of a large amount of money. In reality, he had only a couple of pounds, the remainder being in the form of a cheque. Obviously, a potential robber would not have known of this fact.

However, the police were of the opinion that the attack was a revenge one. This latter theory was supported by Mrs McLaren's statement, in which she said that in the time between her husband leaving the cottage and returning with help, she had never lost consciousness and that no-one entered the house.

As each day passed, the police scaled down their search for both culprit and weapon. They had to agree with the considered opinion that no matter how quickly and effectively their roadblocks had been set up, the killer had escaped their net. The only nagging doubt that lingered was the possibility that the outrageous crime was committed by someone local.

An opinion was voiced that due to the nature of the crime committed, it could have been the act of some escaped lunatic or a recently released madman. The police had considered this possibility and having investigated, dismissed it. On hearing the rumours, they acted quickly in issuing a statement so as to allay the fears of the general public. The manner in which the statement was worded leaves no room for debate on the matter. The statement read 'There are no boarded out imbeciles in the district, as there are in several other rural parts of Scotland'.

On the Wednesday following the shooting, what was heralded as a major breakthrough in the case was reported. Two officers from Ayrshire hurried to Glasgow, and such was their haste that everyone with an interest in the case thought that an arrest was imminent. When the officers returned home without a suspect in custody, these hopes were dashed. But what had caused this urgent dash to Glasgow? Simply an incident that had occurred in the Govanhill area of the city when a 26-year-old man had shot and killed his girlfriend, who had spurned and mocked his advances. He then turned the weapon on himself and shot himself dead. The likelihood of the young man's involvement lessened when it was discovered that the weapon used was of a different calibre to that fired at Portencross.

Less than a month after the murder, on 14th November, the *Glasgow Herald* newspaper published an appeal for information. The notice offered a £100 reward for information leading to an arrest. However, nothing ever came of this appeal and the matter was gradually allow to fade from the public's mind.

McLaren took every opportunity to publicly deride the efforts of the police investigators, calling them incompetent and lazy, amongst other names. It would appear from this behaviour that he had a short fuse attached to his temper.

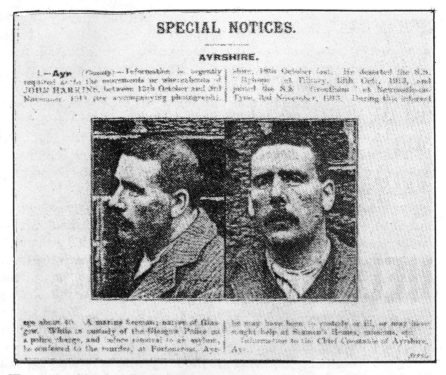

The poster asking for information on the movements of prime suspect John Harkins

Eventually, the inquiry ground to a halt. The police had no suspects and very little in the way of evidence. They had six spent bullets and a set of footprints. They did not even have a description of anyone thought to be remotely involved.

In May 1914, the Portencross Murder sensationally took a new turn. John Harkins, a 40-year-old Glaswegian, walked into his local police office in the Govan area of the city and confessed to the crime. He was detained and officers from Ayrshire interviewed him.

They discovered that Harkins was a merchant seaman who had jumped ship in London on 13th October, five days before the murder. He later sailed from Newcastle aboard the *Greatham* on 3rd November. Yet no matter how many times he was asked, Harkins failed to provide the police with a motive.

Although his home was searched on more than one occasion, nothing of any relevance to the case was found and it was not until a full six months later, in October, that he was finally eliminated from the inquiry. He did not walk free however as he was committed to a lunatic asylum.

As 1914 continued, no fresh clues were forthcoming. By August, other serious events on a world-wide scale were making news, until December, when a local newspaper carried a story under the headline, 'Sequel to Portencross Murder'.

The *Ayr Advertiser* of 14th December 1914 reported that a civil action for damages resulting from an alleged case of slander had been withdrawn at Kilmarnock Sheriff Court. The action had been brought by an Elizabeth Gibson, who was the owner of Portencross Boarding House, and she was seeking £1,000 damages after McLaren had stated that 'she had participated in or had guilty knowledge of the murder of his sister-in-law, Mary Gunn'.

From the information available, it would appear that the McLarens and Mrs Gibson had been friends prior to the murder. However, Mrs Gibson's husband lived most of the time in Glasgow, due to business commitments, and she had taken up with a 24-year-old Glasgow University law student named Finlay Urquhart.

McLaren found this behaviour distasteful and the friendship between the families waned. For whatever reason, best known to himself, McLaren, while on one of his farm business trips, called on Mr Gibson in Glasgow and informed him of the scandalous matter. This resulted in Mr Gibson beginning divorce proceedings.

Of course, Mrs Gibson was more than a little upset that her husband had found out about her infidelity and publicly blamed McLaren for interfering in her life. After the shooting, McLaren was often quoted as saying that he believed the murder was committed by Mrs Gibson's lover—Finlay Urquhart.

So who did commit murder that wet and windy October night in a remote part of Scotland? The police have never charged anyone with the crime and the case still remains open today.

Was it an unknown robber or could it have been someone like Harkins? Now that it is known that McLaren did indeed have enemies, was it someone hell-bent on revenge? There seems to be no doubt that McLaren was the intended target as his wife and sister-in-law were shot only when they stood up and put themselves into the firing line.

On the night of the murder, Finlay Urquhart was staying at Mrs Gibson's boarding house, which was about two minutes' walk from Northbank, or even shorter if running. Could that be the reason why the police saw no one on the road and their roadblocks failed to snare a suspect? Could it be that the murderer never even left the village?

Seven
MYSTERIOUS LIGHTS

Mysterious events can occur at any time and in any place. Whether these incidents happen in our cities or in the countryside makes little difference, as the mystery normally evolves because there are no conclusive clues left behind or, more importantly, no one is present at the time who can later provide an eye-witness account.

What makes the following story all the more mysterious is that there were potentially hundreds of witnesses at or near the scene but not one is certain what they saw.

At the start of the final year of World War I in 1918, Rosyth Naval Base on the Fife side of the Firth of Forth became even busier than usual. Battleships, light and heavy cruisers, destroyers and all manner of support vessels clamoured for any available berthing dock. The throng of ships was swelled by the December order that two flotillas of K-Class submarines, normally based at Scapa Flow in the Orkney Islands, should be re-assigned to Rosyth. The official excuse given for the move was that it was for tactical reasons. The truth of the matter was a little more complicated than that.

Life for a submariner aboard a K-Class submarine was not a posting to be welcomed with open arms. This type of submarine was a relatively new design and, at this time, it was the largest and fastest submarine in the world. Unfortunately, the vessels were also prone to accident.

Shortly after arriving at Rosyth, one of the submarines, K-4, received a VIP on board for a morale-boosting visit. He was the soon-to-be Duke of York and the future King George VI. In an exercise designed to show the Royal visitor the capabilities the monster submarines possessed, K-4 set off from the dockyard and into the Forth.

Another voyage for K-4 comes to an eventful end.

Not very far from shore, the submarine dived and immediately buried her bows in the sea bed. Her stern stuck up above the surface, the propellers rotating wildly in the air.

K-4 remained in this position for over 20 minutes before enough ballast tanks were blown to free her and she scurried back to port. The rest of the Royal visit was cancelled as the future monarch, deeply shocked at his brush with death, made his excuses and departed.

The main problem with the K-Boats, as they were known, was that they were steam driven! The vessels had funnels on the after deck, which had to be closed with watertight hatches every time the submarine wanted to submerge. Once under the surface, they reverted to electric motors for power, fuelled by rows and rows of batteries. In all, each K-Boat had almost 30 openings or vents that had to be securely sealed prior to submerging.

Earlier, on 29th January 1917, K-13 had been launched from Fairfield's shipyard on the Clyde and was undergoing her acceptance trials in the Rhu Narrows of the Gareloch, when she carried out a dive. She sank to the bottom as a result of one of her hatches being inadvertently left open, which flooded the boiler room, killing 32 men. Not until almost three days later was she brought to the surface and the remaining 46 crew and shipyard workers scrambled out of her.

During the time she was lying on the sea-bed, the Admiralty took the strange decision to re-name her. She sank as K-13 and was raised as K-22. Never before, or since, has a vessel had its name changed while sunk. As K-22, she was returned to Fairfield's, re-fitted and eventually took her place in the fleet, where she was to play a major role in the mysterious events in the Forth estuary, a year to the day later.

Due to their poor record, K-Class submarines were rarely used in combat roles. Even though almost every captain of the individual submarines was, in his own way, a dedicated and experienced sub-mariner, whose exploits in earlier models of submarine had made him an ideal candidate for his new command, the K-Boats hardly ever saw action.

All crews aboard submarines were volunteers but not in the sense that they did it from a feeling of duty. By far the majority volunteered because it meant they received a higher rate of pay than those serving on surface ships. This mentality was not confined to the lower ranks either, as one captain of a K-Boat admitted he had volunteered purely because the extra money allowed him to indulge in his expensive hobbies of riding and hunting!

Admiral Beatty, Commander-in-Chief of the Grand Fleet, decided that an exercise would take place in the North Sea. Codenamed Operation E.C.1, Beatty was to lead 26 battleships, 13 cruisers and attendant destroyers, all from the Scapa Flow-based squadrons, while the Rosyth contingent was 3 battleships, 21 cruisers and destroyers with 9 submarines from the 12th and 13th Flotillas, the K-Boats. Each force was to rendezvous somewhere in the North Sea and the battle simulations would begin.

One submarine was missing from the orders and she was K-9. She was earmarked to go to Chatham Dockyard in south-east England, where she was to have new bows fitted. A major problem of having funnels on deck was the ease with which water entered them and put out the boilers. Anything more than a slight swell of the ocean or a sharp turn by the submarine, would inevitably result in an influx of the sea water down the smokestacks. With the boiler fires extinguished, the submarine was left without power and helpless on the surface.

Plans to tackle this ever more common event were drawn up and, one by one, the K-Class boats were to be modified by having swan-shaped bows and funnel extensions fitted, which it was hoped would cure the problem. That this in fact made matters worse as the submarines became more unstable than ever before, did not stop the planned re-fits from continuing.

The real reasons for transferring the K-Flotillas from Scapa Flow to Rosyth are now abundantly clear. The seas around Scapa Flow are notorious for their stormy conditions and, for most of the time, the K-Boats were confined to port. It was hoped that conditions in the calmer waters of the Firth of Forth would stop the sea from invading the submarines.

The inevitable happened to K-9 on the journey south. Just off the coast of Northumberland, she shipped a sea down her funnels and was left with no power. The submarine found herself being tossed about in the middle of a storm and the captain was on the point of giving the order to abandon ship but changed his mind. The cruiser *Southampton*, which was escorting K-9, tried to take her in tow, but twelve men were lost overboard in the attempt to get a line attached to the submarine. K-9 rode out the storm, in the shelter of the cruiser, and was eventually towed to yards in Tyneside for repairs. Although this incident was, in itself, a terrible tragedy, worse was yet to follow in the Forth estuary.

The start of Operation E.C.1 was scheduled for 1st February and it was decided that the Rosyth force would leave their base soon after dark on 31st January. All told, the Rosyth force numbered about 40 vessels, and the organisation of this number of ships negotiating the Firth of Forth, with its minefields, booms and other defences, in the darkness of a cold winter's night, would have been an achievement in itself. Just to make matters a little more difficult, the orders stipulated that radio silence was to be maintained at all times and no vessels were to show any navigational lights apart from a small blue light at the stern, which, in any case, was to be hooded and lit only at half power!

The cruiser *Ithuriel* was instructed to leave Rosyth early with the five submarines of the 13th Flotilla, and to anchor at a place in the estuary known as Burntisland Roads. This order was designed to stagger the starting points of the Battle Force and also ease any possible congestion that might build up.

About 3.30 p.m. that day, Vice Admiral Evan-Thomas, Commander-in-Chief of the Rosyth force, received word that a sea-plane had made contact with a German U-boat that was running on the surface about 5 miles off May Island at the mouth of the Forth. The enemy vessel had submerged before it could be attacked and its present whereabouts were unknown.

Evan-Thomas elected to continue with his plans for the deployment of the Battle Force, although he issued orders that his vessels were to travel at a greater speed than first agreed, so that if the U-boat

Battlecruisers Indomitable, Australia *and* New Zealand *leaving Rosyth.*

was still in the area, it would have a more difficult time hitting a target.

About 6.30 p.m. that night, the assembled squadrons cast off simultaneously from their various berths and moved down the river. The cruiser *Courageous* led the way, followed by *Ithuriel* and her five charges, K-11, K-17, K-14, K-12 and K-22, all travelling in single file about 400 yards apart. Back at Rosyth, battlecruisers *Australia*, *New Zealand*, *Indomitable* and *Inflexible* steamed out, followed by the light cruiser *Fearless*, who was leading the four submarines of the 12th Flotilla, K-4, K-3, K-6 and K-7.

The first hurdle to be overcome by the fleet was Black Rock Gate, which was the opening in the inner defence boom that stretched six miles across the Forth between Leith and Burntisland. Eight minutes after entering this gateway, the force ran into some light fog which reduced visibility to less than 1,000 yards in places.

In an attempt to catch sight of their leader, lost in the fog, the *Ithuriel* and her five submarines increased their speed to 19 knots, but still they could not see the *Courageous*. At this speed, the vessels passed through the Fidra Gap Gate, which was the final obstacle to be cleared before the open North Sea. The gate was the opening in the outer defence boom which stretched for 15 miles between Fidra Island at North Berwick and Elie Ness in Fife.

Just beyond the last defence boom lay May Island, which during war-time was the first defence post for the Forth estuary. On the island was a naval base from which eight trawlers, converted into armed minesweepers, operated. They daily swept the mouth of the estuary, keeping the shipping channels free from danger.

On reaching the island, and obeying their orders, the cruisers increased their speed to 21 knots. At the same time, Commander Harbottle, on the bridge of K-14, peered into the mist and formed the impression that the two K-Boats in front of him were reducing rather than increasing their speed. Not only that, but the leading submarine, K-11, was running off course.

Before he could order any change in speed or direction, the submarine 400 yards in front of him, K-17, mirrored the actions of K-11. As Harbottle ordered a cut in his vessel's speed, he stared as hard as he could into the fog for an answer. Within a minute, he spotted two dark outlines of small ships about half a mile directly ahead of him.

As K-14 closed on the unknown ships, they suddenly switched on their navigation lights and Harbottle realised quickly that he was on a collision course with them. He ordered his helmsman to put the submarine hard to one side and the command was instantly obeyed. Unfortunately, the seaman operating the wheel immediately had to inform his captain that the rudder had jammed and he was unable to free it. The next order from Harbottle was to slow both engines. K-14 then broke with the exercise orders and switched on her full navigational lighting in order to alert following vessels in the convoy of her plight. With almost a full lock on the jammed helm, she would slowly sail round in circles.

The next submarine behind, K-12, had spotted the crippled K-14's lights and in turn, switched on her own. Thanks to the early warning, K-12 passed safely to the rear of K-14. Now, Harbottle had one major worry, and that was how to get out of the way of the following battleships which were about 4 miles upriver from him. As he attempted a manoeuvre, the rudder somehow freed itself, giving the vessel back its steering capabilities, but he had been sailing in a circle for almost six minutes.

Harbottle decided to resume his original course and gave orders to do this. Unfortunately for him and his crew, K-22, the last of the group, had not yet passed and had also lost sight of everyone else in the fog. As K-14 got on course, K-22 steamed out of the mist, and at a speed of 19 knots, sliced into her sister ship, cutting away most of her bows. Two seamen aboard K-14 were killed instantly in the collision. The damage on K-14 was extensive, but limited by the quick-thinking crew members who closed all watertight doors, stopping the inrush of sea from flooding through the rest of the vessel.

On K-22, Captain de Burgh broke radio silence and sent a message in Morse code to the *Ithuriel*. It read: 'Priority. Have been in a collision with submarine K-12. Both ships are flooded forward'. In the confusion and the mist, de Burgh thought he had struck K-12, when in fact he had dealt the damaging blow to K-14, which had, as a result, lost all power.

By now, it was 7.15 p.m. and both submarines sat motionless in the calm, black waters of the river. K-22 was displaying a line of makeshift bright lights strung across the rear of her conning tower, while K-14's signalman was continually blinking out distress calls on his Aldis signalling lamp. Another seaman was regularly firing flares from a Very pistol and the red glow from them reflected eerily in the mist.

The four heavy cruisers of the 2nd Battle Squadron and their numerous escorting destroyers were closing on the scene at a fast 21 knots. The lookouts aboard the first ship, *Australia*, saw the flares from the Very pistol and faintly made out the line of lights strung around the superstructure of K-22.

The men on both submarines could see the approaching outline of the battlecruiser *Australia*, but fortunately, she passed a safe distance away. The others flashed past on either side of the stricken K-Boats and their wash rocked the submarines violently. It seemed that disaster was being averted by a miracle until out of the mist thundered the massive bows of the 22,000-ton *Inflexible*, which had lost all contact with the other vessels in the convoy. The huge cruiser steamed into K-22 and totally bent the submarine's bows back at right angles to the rest of the boat. The *Inflexible* continued without stopping, running over K-22 and pushing her below the surface. As the cruiser disappeared into the mist, K-22 bounced back to the surface, just like a cork, her watertight doors, secured earlier, having held firm.

The *Ithuriel*, by now well out of the estuary, had received the distress call from K-22 and decoded it. The captain, Commander Ernest Leir, had to make an important decision. Could he risk turning round and heading back up river into the path of the fleet or should he ignore the cries for assistance? Leir decided to take the former option, but instructed what was left of his command to turn round slowly and on a wide arc, so as to take them out of the path of the remainder of the convoy.

As they carried out this manoeuvre, K-12 found herself directly in the path of the cruiser *Australia*. Only emergency avoiding action prevented a collision, although the large vessel scraped along the submarine's length, brushing her aside like a little piece of wood with the wash from her propellers. The two squadrons zig-zagged their own way through each other's formations in the darkness, and by sheer good fortune, managed to avoid any further collisions.

But the nightmare was not over. The last part of the convoy, *Fearless* and her four K-Boats, with attendant destroyers and battleships, was coming closer. The distress calls had been received on board this flotilla, but not the information that the *Ithuriel* and three of her submarines were on a return course. The inevitable happened and the two flotillas careered into each other.

Fearless thundered into K-17, her huge bows slicing into the hull just in front of the conning tower. But rather than being pushed under, K-17 was pushed to the side and bobbed and bounced along the whole length of the cruiser. The cold waters of the river poured into the hole in her side as the men below began scrambling up and out onto the deck.

K-17 was sinking slowly by the bow and the escaping crew gathered at the stern, which rose steadily out of the water as each minute passed. Eventually, the men had no option but to take to the water as K-17 slipped noiselessly below the surface. With numerous vessels in the area, it was thought that it would only be a matter of minutes before they were rescued.

By now the night air was echoing to the sound of many klaxons ringing out their alarms. K-4 and K-3, behind, immediately stopped their engines. Again, the lumbering leviathans took an age to stop completely. K-3 sailed past K-4 with the sound of scraping as they brushed together, eventually coming to a complete halt some distance beyond.

The third submarine, K-6, at one point was bearing down on K-12, which only minutes before had escaped being sunk by the *Australia*. Again, emergency avoiding action was taken and a collision was averted, but only momentarily. As K-6 veered away from K-12, she pushed her bows almost dead centre into the stationary K-4. K-6 had been the first vessel fitted with the new strengthened swan-shaped bows, and these cut through K-4's pressured hull with relative ease. The blow was to prove fatal as K-4 was forced over and onto her side and began to sink immediately.

The extensive damage to HMS Fearless *after colliding with and sinking K-17.*
(Imperial War Museum)

Still the drama was not at an end. K-6's bows were firmly embedded in the hull of the dying submarine and as she slowly sank, she was pulling K-6 under with her. Full reverse engines were applied immediately and a deadly game of push and pull continued for only two or three minutes, but what seemed to the crew of the violently rocking and thrashing K-6 to be an eternity. One final thrust of her engines and K-6 lurched out of K-4's grasp and back from the brink of disaster. Now free, K-4 began to slip further down in the water, just as K-7 came up from behind. She had stopped her engines and was slowly coming to a halt.

Silently, she loomed out of the mist, scraped along the side of K-6 and then gently nudged the bow of K-4, almost as if in a farewell gesture. K-4 sank to the bottom of the estuary. Not one member of her crew escaped. All of this happened within yards of where K-17 had sunk minutes earlier, and where her crew members still floundered in the icy waters.

By now, every vessel in the fleet was aware of the original coded message sent by K-22. As the very last part of the convoy arrived on the scene, the battleships and assorted destroyers sailed through the groups of stationary submarines. They ran over the men in the water, churning up or pulling under most of the 56 crew members of K-17 who were waiting for rescue. Only nine men were taken from the river alive, and one later died from his injuries.

The final reckoning was that K-4 and K-17 had been sunk. K-14, K-6 and K-22 were seriously damaged, while *Ithuriel* and *Fearless* had sustained damage to their bows. For the Rosyth force, Operation E.C.1 was over before it began, and the vessels which had so proudly sailed less than three hours beforehand, now slowly limped or were towed back to port. 103 sailors were killed, not one of them as a result of enemy action.

An Admiralty Court of Inquiry was called for and quickly convened on 4th February. It was held on board the battleship *Orion* at the Rosyth base and it took evidence from all those involved. Once the testimony relating to who had collided with whom was heard, it was apparent to all present that there were mysterious circumstances involved that needed to be explained. Only some of the mysteries were solved.

One question that required an answer was why had it taken almost an hour for *Ithuriel* to receive and decode K-22's distress call. Perhaps this mystery is the easiest of all to explain. When first received and decoded, K-22's call was to the effect that K-12 had been in a collision with a steamer named *Nova Scotia*.

The official reason given for this incorrect message was that either the signalman on K-22 or the wireless operator on the *Ithuriel* was using the wrong code! It was not until 20 minutes after this message was received that a second one came in, this time with the right message. At this point, it was a full hour after the original collision, but the communication gave no details of the time of the incident. Commander Leir, now in receipt of the facts, decided at this stage to turn his flotilla around.

The second mystery is what had caused the steering to jam on K-14. Thomas Gardener, engineer Lieutenant on K-14, told the Inquiry that while bringing that vessel back to port after the disaster, he had deliberately tried to re-create the conditions under which the steering had jammed on the submarine, but he failed to do it. Every manoeuvre he tried failed to lock up the steering. Back in port, K-14 was lifted out of the water and naval and civilian engineers inspected the whole steering system but could not find any faults with it. So what had caused it to jam—and at such a critical time? This question was never satisfactorily answered by the Inquiry and a solution to this mystery still remains elusive to this day.

The final and greatest mystery of all, and that which led to all the other incidents and mysteries, was the identity of the two ships whose lights were seen. The Inquiry heard from officers and men of the convoy who had seen the lights of the ships. There is also some evidence that suggests that the lights of more than two ships were seen. The popular assumption was, and it still exists in some people's minds, that the lights were those of the minesweeper flotilla from May Island.

Three captains from the minesweeper group, along with their commanding officer, Captain Robinson Rigby, were called to give evidence to the Inquiry. They each stated that although they had been out in the estuary that night, they had not been operating in the area where the disasters occurred. They heard and saw nothing out of the ordinary. As their operating logs were available to the Inquiry for inspection, this evidence has to be believed.

What did come to notice though was that the minesweeper detachment had never been told about the plans to have 40 ships of the Grand Fleet moving down the Forth during the hours of darkness. That they should have been told was never in doubt. Someone in authority at the Rosyth base simply forgot to tell them!

So, if the lights were not those of the minesweepers, then who did they belong to? Some thought that they might have belonged to a number of German U-boats hunting together, but that idea can be discounted for obvious reasons. Not one shot was fired, and U-boats would certainly not be showing lights, navigational or otherwise.

The riddle of the mystery lights was never solved. Although there is absolutely no evidence to support the following suggestion, it is one that regularly occurs in conversations about this incident. Could the operating logs of the minesweeper flotilla have been altered to read that it was nowhere near the area of the disaster?

The simple response to this suggestion of criminal falsification of records is another question, and that is why the officers of the minesweepers should have thought this action necessary. They had not been told of the Rosyth fleet's intended movements, and therefore could not be held responsible in any way.

The Inquiry concluded after five days on 9th February 1918. It failed to come up with any reasonable answers to some of the mysteries surrounding the incident and instead chose to look for scapegoats. No consideration was ever given to the fact that the K-Boats were not designed or intended for use with the rest of the Grand Fleet. This disaster proved beyond doubt that there was no way they could work in close proximity with other battle vessels or, for that matter, with other submarines.

The Inquiry's report to Admiral Beatty was nothing more than a whitewash designed to exonerate, at all costs, the majority of those commanding the surface ships, by laying the blame for all the collisions on the shoulders of four of the K-Boat captains. Commander Ernest Leir of the *Ithuriel* was also blamed, and later he was the only one to be court-martialled over the affair, although the charge against him was found 'not proven'. Those K-Boat commanders who were blamed did not have to face a similar indignity or blemish on their records, but were simply moved to different commands.

After this mysterious tragedy, most of the K-Boats were either lost through further accidents or saw out the remainder of the war in safe waters. If any of them ever saw an enemy vessel, it was usually from a great distance. On one of the rare occasions when a K-Boat engaged the enemy, in April 1918, it came about by chance. Captain Kellet of K-7 fired a torpedo at a German U-boat. His aim was accurate and it hit the enemy vessel almost in the centre, but true to form, the torpedo was a dud and failed to explode. The enemy submarine managed to escape with hardly a dent in its metal to show for the encounter. By 1926, the last K-Boat was in the scrapyard.

The following remark, made by Commander Leir, who reached the rank of Rear Admiral before retiring, so that it appears being court-martialled did not interrupt his successful career too much, just about sums it all up. In an interview given in 1961, he said, 'The only good thing about K-Boats was that they never engaged the enemy'.

K-4 and K-17 lie at the bottom of the Forth, the wrecks officially classed as war graves. Spare a thought for the brave men who lie within the now rusted hulks, victims of a still-mysterious series of events which became known as 'the Battle of May Island'.

Eight
A ROYAL TRAGEDY ... OR COVER-UP?

Scotland's adverse weather has featured in many of the most horrific accidents, disasters and tragedies that have befallen our nation in past years. Indeed, even in this book, in half of the chapters, nature's elements play their part, whether it be in a major role or otherwise. Perhaps the influence that hostile weather conditions exert is severely misjudged, for it seems that when they are involved, the mystery invariably becomes all the greater.

At the start of World War II, Oban, thanks to its natural sheltered position on the west coast of the mainland and its excellent communication network, was selected as suitable for the location of a front-line RAF Coastal Command Station. Its aircraft, all of them flying boats, were to patrol the North Atlantic on missions aimed at keeping the waters of the Northern Approaches safe from lurking enemy U-boats, monitoring convoy movements and taking part in search and rescue operations. The air crews who flew the flying boats were a truly international force, with men from all corners of the world in their ranks. Unfortunately, the turnover in personnel of Coastal Command was abnormally high due to the large number of losses compared to some other branches of the RAF.

In March 1942, as part of the natural rotation of squadrons around the various bases, no. 228 Squadron brought their Sunderland aircraft to Oban from Stranraer. Unbeknown to anyone at this time, one of their planes was to feature later that year in a major mystery of the War.

Flight Lieutenant Frank McKenzie Goyen, an Australian from the state of Victoria, although only 25 years of age, was one of the most experienced pilots on the base with thousands of flying hours to his credit. His aircraft, a Mark III Sunderland with the call sign W-4026, had a crew of ten, all of them experienced in operational matters. The youngest, 20-year-old rear gunner, Flight Sergeant Andrew Jack, was a Grangemouth lad. His father was a foreman docker in his home town, a well-known semi-professional footballer who was proud of his son's achievement in defending his country.

On Sunday 23rd August 1942, six months into their tour of duty at Oban and after flying hundreds of missions, the crew of W-4026 were given a break from fighting the war and instructed to fly their plane to the RAF base at Invergordon on the Dornoch Firth, where they were to uplift a special passenger.

The Sunderland took off from Oban and followed the length of the Caledonian Canal until reaching its destination. Although this was probably the shortest route in any case, Goyen was following instructions that a flying boat should always attempt to route any journey over water. Perhaps one reason behind this was that these types of aircraft were notorious for their slow rate of climb, the maximum being about 200 feet a minute, and therefore they were not particularly agile. They were, after all, flying boats, and not really suitable for use in the mountainous areas of the Highlands.

On arrival at Invergordon, the crew discovered that their VIP passenger was to be His Royal Highness, the Duke of Kent, brother of the King. In his capacity as Air Commodore in the Department of the Inspector General, the Duke had been given the task of visiting RAF bases and interviewing the flight crews and ground staff, listening and noting their grievances or otherwise and thereafter reporting his findings to the Air Ministry. With hindsight, it was probably nothing more than a round of Royal visits designed to keep up the morale of the men at the sharp end. After all, here was a member of the Royal family in military uniform doing his bit for the war effort. It gave the right impression to the public at large that no one was exempt from pulling together to defeat the enemy.

As their distinguished passenger was not due to arrive at Invergordon until Tuesday, the early arrival of W-4026 gave the crew time to relax and enjoy their surroundings. Many old acquaintances were met in the mess and stories of earlier exploits told and re-told. Goyen's crew, like almost every other, had varying backgrounds. Counting himself, it consisted of three Australians, one New Zealander and seven British. Irrespective of their differences, everyone

Flight Lt. Frank Goyen at the controls of his Sunderland Mk. III aircraft.
(228 Squadron Association)

now had a common purpose and enemy.

The Duke of Kent and his entourage of three others arrived in Inverness early on Tuesday morning, 25th August 1942, from the overnight sleeper train from London, and he was driven the last few miles to Invergordon. He had instructions to visit the RAF base at Reykjavik on Iceland, a place he had been to before. After meeting with Goyen, he was introduced to the crew members, who included Wing Commander Thomas L. Moseley, another Australian who, as the Commanding Officer of 228 Squadron, had invited himself along and would be acting as co-pilot on this trip, bringing the total crew number to eleven.

Once everyone was safely on board, the Sunderland began her taxi-ing in the Firth. Unusually, on this day the sea was flat calm and the flying boat thundered along the surface for longer than usual, carrying 15 personnel, over 2,500 gallons of fuel and a full payload of munitions. Goyen was looking ahead for any sign of even a small wave that he might be able to use, like a ramp, to give his plane a final push into the air. Eventually, after about three miles, the huge aircraft gained air under its belly and slowly began to climb into the sky. It was 1.10 p.m.

At this point, the first mystery arises. There are no copies of the W-4026 flight plan available today. This was not a flight plan filed by the pilot, but one that had been made up for him to follow and was therefore part of his orders. That such a thing existed there is no doubt, because it was later referred to in official correspondence, but what happened to it, and the official orders, can only be guessed at.

The usual flight path for an aircraft flying to Iceland was for it to follow the coastline north to the Pentland Firth, then turn west and head for the Faroe Islands and thereafter the ultimate destination. It was planned in this manner so that as usual, the plane would be flying over water at all times. Only in emergencies were flights allowed to cut across the corner of this part of the mainland, and then only when north of Wick, where there are no mountains as such, only hills of medium height.

Fifteen minutes into the journey, the Sunderland hit a mixture of cloud and dense fog. However, this had been expected, thanks to the accurate weather forecasts from the base at Invergordon. These reports also mentioned that the foul weather was localised, as the Pentland Firth was in clear conditions. W-4026 flew on in the fog blind, using her instruments to calculate height, speed and direction, and what happened in the next five to fifteen minutes no-one can say with absolute certainty.

Between 1.30 and 1.40 p.m., the Sunderland was heard droning its way lazily above a river valley known as Berriedale Water, which is south of Dunbeath, which in turn is south of Wick. The noise of its Bristol Pegasus engines startled a number of the locals, who could hear it but could not see it, due to the mist.

The plane continued up the valley and passed to the side of a 2,000-foot high ridge known locally as Donald's Mount. As it lumbered on, slowly losing altitude, the 800-foot high cliff of Eagle's Rock loomed out of the fog. The Sunderland tried hard to climb and turn away from the rising edge of the rock face, the pitch of her engines now a roar, but it was all too late. The aircraft struck the side of the ridge leading to the cliff and cartwheeled a number of times.

The wings broke off as the fuel tanks, almost full, along with the depth charge munitions, exploded and engulfed everything in a massive fireball. Only one man survived the inferno.

At the moment of impact, the rear gun turret had broken off completely from the main fuselage and, like a human cannonball, Andrew Jack found himself being hurled through the air, ensconced in his glass dome, and clear of the explosion. He was badly injured, receiving cuts and gashes from where he had made contact with the broken glass, but although stunned and shocked, he managed to free himself and immediately went towards the crash site.

A Sunderland flying boat similar to W-4026. (228 Squadron Association)

As he staggered around in the debris and choking smoke, he found some of his colleagues lying where they had been thrown clear from the disintegrating aircraft, but when he checked them, each was dead. He could see more of his crew in the burning remains of the plane and tried to reach them, but such was the heat from the fiercely burning wreckage, he was badly burned in his attempts and beaten back. He realised he needed to get help.

Meanwhile, those locals who had heard the Sunderland pass overhead and then the roar of the explosion had raised the alarm, and search parties from numerous local communities were quickly assembled. Due to the remoteness of the crash site, about 8 miles from Dunbeath, and the low-lying cloud and fog, the search parties took a number of hours to reach the scene. It has been said in previous accounts that the searchers found the mist was so dense at some points that they could only make progress by following the strong smell of aviation fuel that hung in the air.

Eventually, after about three hours, the first would-be rescuers arrived at the crash site. The scene that greeted them was one of almost total devastation. The still smouldering plane was broken into thousands of pieces and scattered over a wide area. Only a part of the tail section survived, which helped identify the wreckage as an aircraft. Melted aluminium had dripped onto the ground and lay cooling in grotesque shapes. Even small rocks and stones in the area were seen to have minute grains of the silver metal fused into them. Bodies lay all around but there was nothing that could be done for them, other than to cover them over with some retrieved parachutes.

In the still and heavy atmosphere that lingered around the scene, one of the searchers, a policeman, thought he could hear a faint voice crying out. Every man fell silent, but after a minute or so, with no further sound heard, the work continued. Within a short space of time, fourteen bodies lay side by side on the wet grass.

A local doctor, Dr John Kennedy, arrived at the scene after most of the bodies had been laid out. His lateness is not surprising when it is learned that he was 70 years of age and had to tramp over more than four miles of fog-bound moorland to reach the site. It was he who recognised the Royal passenger when he pulled back the make-shift shroud of parachute silk.

Unlike some others of the crew, the face of the Duke was, apart from a huge gash on the forehead, relatively unmarked, but what confirmed his identity beyond doubt for the doctor was the bracelet on the body's wrist. It was inscribed, 'His Royal Highness, The Duke of Kent, The Coppins, Iver, Buckinghamshire'.

Word was immediately sent to the authorities at the RAF base at Wick. Due to the lateness of the hour and the remote location of the site, nothing more could be done that day. A guard was mounted overnight by the police at the scene to prevent any unauthorised spectators getting close. The following day, RAF and Army personnel were brought in and took charge, their first job being to remove the bodies from the hillside.

As this was going on, Andrew Jack stumbled over a fence and into the garden of a cottage almost three miles from the crash site. It had taken him almost 23 hours to reach this point, mainly because of his serious injuries. His face and hands were badly blistered due to his burns and the blood from his wounds had congealed in the places where earlier it had found a path to run. His flying suit was torn to pieces and he had lost his boots.

The woman of the house found him just before he fell into unconsciousness and he managed to tell her, 'I'm an airman and our plane has crashed. I am the sole survivor'. He was later taken to hospital in Lybster and treated for his many injuries.

A cloak of secrecy was thrown over the whole incident and in the course of the next three weeks, every piece of wreckage from W-4026 was gathered from the hillside by the Army and carted away. The only thing out of place when they had completed their task was a 200 yards long by 100 yards wide gouge in the grass, and an even wider band which had been scorched black by the flames.

Andrew Jack was visited in hospital by senior RAF officers and told not to say anything about the incident. He was informed that this was necessary as he would be required as a witness at a forthcoming Court of Inquiry. Yet, when the Inquiry was held, headed by Wing Commander Warren Kay, it gave rise to two mysteries. First, the papers detailing the Inquiry's findings have vanished. There is no trace of them at either the Public Record Office at Kew, the RAF Air Historical Branch or the Royal Archives at Windsor Castle. More surprising is the second mystery, namely why Andrew Jack was never called to give evidence to the Inquiry. He would no doubt have had vital information to relate, being the only eye-witness to the tragedy, but he was never given the chance to tell his story.

Some of the Inquiry's findings were later made public, however, in a roundabout way. On 7th October of that year, the Air Minister Sir Archibald Sinclair spoke in the House of Commons on the tragic death of the Duke of Kent. Part of his speech dealt with the Inquiry's report. He said:

> The Court of Inquiry found; first, that the accident occurred because the aircraft was flown on a track other than that indicated on the flight plan given to the pilot and at too low an altitude to clear the rising ground on the track; secondly, that the responsibility for this serious mistake in airmanship lies with the captain of the aircraft; thirdly, that the weather encountered should have presented no difficulty to an experienced pilot; fourthly, that the examination of the propellers showed that the engines were under power when the aircraft struck the ground...

The Inquiry was unequivocal in its conclusion. The accident was due to 'pilot error' and therefore the blame was apportioned to Frank Goyen. The official findings provoked quite a murmur of discontent, but at this time, only in the ranks of the other crews of Coastal Command. Those who voiced their displeasure at the result, did so sure in the knowledge that this was no ordinary 'accident'.

These were the same men who flew Sunderlands day in and day out and who were acutely aware of the problems of piloting the cumbersome flying boats. They also knew that over 80 similar aircraft had been lost in one type of accident or another, but only two of them as the result of direct enemy action. To them, the blaming of the dead pilot for making an error which resulted in the loss of the aircraft and fourteen lives, was the easy option for the Inquiry.

Two months after the speech in Parliament, the matter came to the fore again. In December 1942, a communiqué from the German

Embassy in Lisbon, Portugal, to the German Foreign Minister in Berlin was intercepted. The message suggested that W-4026 had been sabotaged, not by German agents, but by British Intelligence, as the Duke of Kent had been considered by some to be a secret sympathiser with Nazi ideals. This is an excellent example of the reporting of rumour and counter-rumour. Irrespective of whether or not it was true, it was hoped that Berlin could make something out of it for propaganda purposes.

Indeed, it has previously been well documented that if Hitler had managed to conquer Britain, then his plan was to install a new monarch, purely as a figurehead. Among the many named as possible candidates to become the puppet king was the former ruler, Edward VIII, now Governor of the Bahamas, and the afore-mentioned Duke of Kent.

However, the idea that fourteen other men on the flight were to be sacrificed appears to be totally absurd and extremely callous. Yet those who subscribe to this theory simply say that the crew were chosen because they held the same sympathies as the Duke.

In reality, there is absolutely no truth in this suggestion. If proof were needed, then take the case of Andrew Jack, who later returned to duty and was eventually transferred with 228 Squadron to another RAF base in Northern Ireland, where he gained promotion. It hardly needs to be said that this is not the recognised way of dealing with a suspected sympathiser to the German cause. Some mischief makers suggested that Jack's elevation in rank was a thank-you from the hierarchy for keeping quiet. More likely he earned the extra pay because he was the most experienced man for the job.

Andrew Jack never publicly aired his opinion on the findings, but he is reported to have privately remarked to his sister that whatever had caused the accident it certainly was not 'pilot error'. He obviously felt deep regret that he had been sworn to secrecy and that his dead friend Frank Goyen was now being blamed for the crash. However, their friendship added to the mysteries when it became known that on the day of the fatal flight, Goyen handed an inscribed photograph of himself to Jack bearing the words 'In memory of happier times'.

Over the intervening years, a lot of mystery has attached itself to this gesture. Did Goyen know something the others did not? Perhaps all he had was a premonition that something terrible was going to happen, like so many others have had prior to tragedies occurring. Was it part of his premonition or sheer coincidence that he should present it to the one member of his crew who was to survive what was soon to befall them?

Amateurs and experts alike have long theorised on the possible scenarios leading up to the crash on Eagle's Rock. There is no argument that the plane was off course, by about 13 degrees, which is quite a substantial miscalculation in a flight that only lasted half an hour or less and flew a distance of no more than 50 miles, but there may be a logical explanation for this.

The Mark III version Sunderland had been fitted with new technology. The aircraft had a distant reading gyro magnetic compass fitted in the bowels of the fuselage. It was as far away as possible from the cockpit area, whose magnetic mass could not then interfere with the correct working of the compass. Yet, because of the difference between true north and magnetic north, the new equipment still required to be manually set by the navigator before each flight, to take account of the variation.

The interesting point among all this technical jargon is that at Invergordon, the magnetic variation was 13 degrees west of true north—exactly the same amount W-4026 was off course when it struck Eagle's Rock. Could it be that someone—the navigator—simply forgot to set the new compass prior to take-off?

If the compass was correctly set before departure, then there must be another reason for W-4026 veering off course. One explanation put forward for discussion seems to be the most plausible, purely because the same circumstances had happened so many times before and since the Duke's final flight.

The theory is that the Sunderland was, while in flight, being gently blown by side winds, which each minute were pushing it more and more towards land. The compass in the cockpit would still be giving the correct bearing but not the true position and as they were flying in thick weather, the crew could not see that they were over land and not water. The first intimation they got of this fatal miscalculation was when they spied the fast approaching cliff face of Eagle's Rock.

However, as this particular flight was of a short duration, the side winds would need to have been of a speed approaching 50 m.p.h. for the aircraft to have veered so far off course. This is hardly 'being gently blown' or 'being blown unnoticeably', as has also been suggested in the past. In fact, the records show that very little wind was recorded that day.

After all the conjecture, it would appear that the final flight of W-4026 ended, just as the Inquiry found, because of a combination of errors, which were either unknown or ignored by those on board. Yet, for some reason, the tragedy would not allow itself to be forgotten.

Andrew Jack died in 1978. Before this, he may have further opened the neck of the bag holding the mystery by saying that during the flight of W-4026 he had been instructed to drop some smoke floats, which were designed to show the crew just how much, if any, side wind was present. Jack had a smoke float sight in his gun turret, and by looking through it, he would be able to gauge the drift of the smoke and thereafter calculate the speed of the winds. This information would be transferred to the pilot, who could then make adjustments in his course to compensate for any drift of his aircraft.

Jack did as he was instructed and immediately radioed back to the pilot that he had done so. He awaited acknowledgement of his transmission and when it came, he was surprised to realise that he did not recognise the voice on the intercom. This statement is from a man who knew all of the other crew members and his Squadron Commander well. So who owned the mystery voice on the radio? Who was it in the pilot's seat that answered Jack's call of 'Skipper, I've dropped the smoke floats'?

Perhaps the answer to the puzzle of the mystery voice lies in another alleged remark, this time made by a special constable who was a member of the first search party to arrive at the crash site, and which has only been revealed since his death. He stated that, contrary to the official report that the Duke of Kent's body was recovered from the hillside, having been thrown clear of the plane wreckage, he had in fact, assisted in removing the Duke's corpse from the pilot's seat!

Did the Duke pull rank and ask to fly the plane after take-off? Was Frank Goyen ordered to hand over the controls of his plane by his Squadron Commander Moseley? Although he had spent the previous ten years in the Royal Navy before taking up his new job, the Duke was an accomplished pilot in his own right. There is eye-witness evidence to say that he had piloted planes whilst on previous visits to other Air Force bases. But experienced as he was, handling a fully-laden Sunderland aircraft, in thick cloud and fog, was totally different to what he was used to. After they entered the foul weather, did events overtake them so quickly that there was no time for Goyen to take back control?

Snippets taken from the statement of Andrew Jack, made in 1942 from his hospital bed to senior air crash investigators from the RAF, suggested that he heard comments on his radio headset from someone in the cockpit to the effect that they would need to 'go down and have a look'.

While no one will ever know for certain, consider the following as a possible explanation of events. After take-off, the Duke of Kent is asked if he wishes to pilot the aircraft. At this time, the weather is reasonably clear. Jack is ordered to send out some smoke flares and does so. When he radioes this information, the Duke, now in the pilot's seat, acknowledges his message. However, before Jack can obtain a reading from the flares, the Sunderland enters the heavy cloud and fog. By now, any side winds that have been acting on the aircraft and pushing it off course, remain unobserved by any of the crew. As an alternative to this part of the theory, as stated before, the new compass had not been properly set, if at all.

As the crew are unable to see anything, a decision is taken in the cockpit to 'take the plane down and have a look', probably to determine at what ceiling height the fog is lying. This is the radio message that Jack overhears. The manoeuvre of taking the plane lower can be done safely by paying careful attention to the altimeter gauge in the cockpit. If the fog is only at 200 feet and above, the aircraft can fly in the clear weather below it and above the surface of the sea.

As the Sunderland descends through the mist, it is now seriously off course and over land. With the aircraft at a height of about 700 feet, the bluff face of Eagle's Rock, towering even higher, suddenly appears in view and there is no time, not even with the application of full power to all four engines, to take avoiding action to clear the ridge.

Once the authorities found out the true facts, the wheels were set in motion to suppress them. There would have been no mystery if there had been no attempt at a cover-up. It would have been another familiar case of a plane flying into a hillside in fog, albeit on this occasion, a plane with a Royal pilot!

Could this be the real reason why the Registrar of the Royal Archives states that 'the position has not changed with regard to papers here relating to the death of the Duke of Kent: they are not available to researchers'? Are there records in existence that tell the whole truth in the matter, but are still being kept secret, thus perpetuating the mystery of the final flight of W-4026?

Nine
SABOTAGED?

In times of war, sabotage is a tactic employed for one purpose only and that is to cause maximum damage and disruption to the enemy. When successful, and because of the secretive nature of such wartime operations, mysteries inevitably grow out of the events.

During World War II, all branches of the armed forces faced their own crisis points in their respective battlegrounds. Dunkirk and Singapore were demoralising events but four years later the success of the D-Day Normandy landings far outweighed these earlier losses. The Battle of Britain was not only the personal turning point for the Air Force, but also the whole country.

The battle for control of the shipping lanes of the North Atlantic crossings had its share of defeats and victories for the Allies. There were times when a couple of days would not pass without a report of a vessel being sunk as a result of enemy action. Convoy after convoy zig-zagged their courses across the hostile grey expanse of water, the crews never knowing when, or if, their particular vessel might be silhouetted in the periscope sights of an enemy U-boat.

In the end, thanks to the Royal Navy eventually gaining the upper hand, our country was able to re-equip itself with munitions, food and troops from all over the world and bring safely to these shores by ship. But none of the battles fought, even those considered as victories, were without cost.

Unlike other chapters in this book, the mysterious circumstances about to be related cover more than one incident. Each of these incidents can be linked, and in some cases, in more than one way. In the continual striving to make our war equipment better, bigger and more deadly than the enemy's, a large number of servicemen died, not in the hostile atmosphere of a far-off battlefield, but in the testing grounds in and around their homes. There is evidence to suggest that their deaths were not accidental.

Early in 1943, the workforce of the Vickers-Armstrong shipyard at Barrow were putting the finishing touches to a new U-class submarine that had taken shape on their stocks over the last few months. As the crew assembled in the shipyard, ready to take delivery of the new vessel, a strange thing happened. They were told that the submarine was to have its name changed. She was to have been called HMS *Unbridled*, but because she had been modified and upgraded she had now become one of the first in the new V-Class of submarine. She would be renamed HMS *Vandal*.

Most sailors are superstitious and this crew were no exception. More than a few words of discontent were to be heard but it did not come to much, probably because of the fact that out of a total complement of 37 men, only about 15 of them had been on a submarine before!

The captain of the new HMS *Vandal* was Lt. James Bridger. He was an experienced man, as much as anyone can be when aged 25. It was to be his first command. Early on 18th February, *Vandal* left its dock and sailed for the safe waters of the Firth of Clyde, where she would be carrying out her 'working up' exercises.

This 'working up' period is, in effect, a time of trials, during which the crew make sure that all the equipment is in place and working correctly and get to know their new vessel. In the case of the *Vandal*, just like any other new vessel during wartime, the crew had been brought together for the first time and it was a chance for them to get to know each other too. This tradition of trials and exercises continues to this day with all newly-completed naval vessels.

Vandal arrived on the Clyde two days later after an uneventful journey up the west coast and berthed next to HMS *Forth*, the depot ship of the 3rd Submarine Flotilla, whose base was at Dunoon. The new vessel was put through her first trial on the Gareloch and all went well. It was remarked at this stage by one of the officers overseeing the tests that the submarine seemed to him to have fewer, if any, faults than some previous vessels.

As a result of passing the first of her trials, the *Vandal* now proceeded to the next stage of trials and tests. These were to last for three days, during which time the submarine would be on her own. This was designed as a real test for both vessel and crew, when the vessel would sail without the necessity of informing its base of any of its

The only known photograph of HMS Vandal.
(Royal Navy Museum)

movements. Albeit still within the confines of the Clyde, the entire crew could look on it as a simulation of a 'wartime patrol'. For some of them, it was to be a first-time experience.

All appears to have gone well with the exercise for the first two days and nights at least. On the second night, the *Vandal* was observed lying at anchor in the bay just off the town of Lochranza on the island of Arran. While some reports differ over about whether it was the postmaster or the piermaster, whoever it was stated that he had seen the submarine leave early on the Wednesday morning of 24th February. He was able to identify the vessel by the conning tower markings of P.64. This was the *Vandal*.

Her assignment on this third, and last, day, was to complete a deep dive to around 200 feet in the Arran Trench, a passage of water which, in some places, plunges to a depth over 500 feet. The Trench lies south of the mouth of lower Loch Fyne, extending all the way down the east side of Arran and coming to an end in the vicinity of Holy Isle near the southern tip.

Later that day, the *Vandal* failed to report back to HMS *Forth*. It was not until the following day, Thursday 25th February, thanks to a chance remark, that the realisation dawned on the commanding officers of the 3rd Flotilla that one of their submarines was missing. There have been allegations made over the intervening years that even as they ordered the search to begin, they were still not entirely certain which particular submarine it was they were supposed to be trying to locate. Perhaps this claim is a little unfair on the officers of the 3rd Flotilla, considering the circumstances of the trials and also when it is revealed that six other submarines were also exercising in the same area.

However late the search began, clues as to the possible whereabouts of the *Vandal* were reported. With the search area being confined to the area between Inchmarnock, Lochranza and the island of Sgat Mor at the entrance to Loch Fyne, three separate events were reported.

Firstly, a smoke candle was seen in the area of the Lamont Shelf, which lies to the south of Ardlamont Point. A smoke candle is something that is used by submarines and aircraft when they wish to mark a particular spot, and as such is not considered to be a signal of distress. Secondly, a sound similar to that of hull tapping was heard nine cables south of Sgat Mor, which in layman's terms is equivalent to a distance of about half a mile, there being 100 yards in each 'cable'. Lastly, later in the afternoon, the air base at Machrihanish reported that one of its search aircraft had spotted an oil slick about two miles north west of Lochranza.

When all this information was relayed back to the submarine base at Dunoon, a decision was taken to ignore the oil slick and concentrate in the area of the other two sightings. It was felt that if the *Vandal* had encountered problems, it would be during her deep dive in the Arran Trench. The first two reported incidents were within that area, whereas the oil slick was not.

For three days the search continued, until on Saturday 27th February, it was eventually stood down. Not one trace of the *Vandal* had been found. Soon after, a very quick official inquiry was held on board the depot ship *Forth*. As no one knew exactly what had happened to *Vandal*, no satisfactory conclusions came out of it. With so many possible explanations available to them, the inquiry took the sensible decision of refusing to speculate on any possible cause.

As events of the war replaced thoughts of the lost submarine, another tragedy was soon to befall the 3rd Submarine Flotilla just over two months later. On 30th May 1943, HMS *Untamed*, recently launched by the same firm of Vickers-Armstrong as its next submarine completed after *Vandal*, but this time from its shipyard on Tyneside, sank while on similar 'working up' exercises in the sea just off Campbeltown in Argyllshire.

The difference in this case was that the *Untamed*'s sinking was witnessed by her supply ship. The submarine had been travelling just

HMS Untamed, *seen here after her sinking and now renamed HMS* Vitality.
(Royal Navy Museum)

below the surface, getting ready to carry out a dive to periscope depth.
As her superstructure slipped below the waves, she disappeared completely from the view of those on her escorting ship following along-
side. This immediately raised suspicions that something was wrong
because at least part of the submarine should have been visible at all
times. The alarm was raised and rescue operations were begun without delay as the *Untamed* came to rest on the bottom, 150 feet below
the surface.

The crew of the *Untamed* fought for hours inside the stricken submarine in frantic efforts to re-float her, but they were to lose the battle. Water was flooding into the vessel via a piece of equipment known
as the Ottway Log tank. This device was intended to measure the
submarine's speed in the water and was wound by hand through an
opening in the hull.

The Ottway had stuck, leaving a valve open, and the sea waters
rushed into the submarine. Panic set into some crew members and as
they fled along the vessel from one flooded compartment to the next,
they failed to secure the watertight doors behind them. By the time
this mistake was corrected, it was far too late.

Unfortunately, the same panic that had caused excess flooding
had already been responsible for the deaths of two of the crew. They
had been shut off from the rest of the vessel when the watertight
doors were eventually closed.

It gradually became apparent that trying to refloat the submarine was not a viable option and plans were made to effect an escape from the crippled vessel. It was at this time the crew discovered that a large number of oxygen tanks needed for the escape could not be used because they were located in lockers in the already flooded area, which was now closed off.

As the remaining crew members gathered in the engine room, the order was given to flood this part of the submarine. Even then this plan did not work due to a faulty valve which meant that the water only trickled in rather than gushing in at the greater speed expected. The men set frantically to work, using other methods to flood the compartment.

After what must have felt like an eternity, the engine-room filled with water and the escape hatch was opened. As the first man rose slowly upward and through the hatch, a covering lid fell back on top of him and he died instantly. His lifeless body became wedged in the escape hatch, blocking it totally. There was no other way out for the remaining 34 crew. It was only a matter of hours before their oxygen ran out and each and every one of them died.

All during this time, numerous attempts were being made on the surface in an effort to rescue the men but nothing thought of or tried was remotely successful. The rescue operations were also being hampered by severe storms which had sprung up just after the sinking and continued to batter the area for two days non-stop. After three days, the salvage teams were eventually successful in winching the *Untamed* to the surface.

Once the sea waters had been pumped out of the submarine, investigators climbed aboard and slowly moved through the vessel inch by inch. Everywhere inside was silent and covered in grey coloured silt. It was only after the investigators, who were not Navy personnel, had completed their examinations that the bodies of the 37 crew were removed by the crew of the sister vessel, HMS *Untiring*, which had been assisting throughout in the rescue operations.

Once again, a Board of Inquiry was set up at 3rd Flotilla Headquarters. The question of the failed escape attempt was one of the matters investigated by the Inquiry. Evidence was laid before it that the flood valve in the engine room of the *Untamed* had been wrongly fitted and that this had been the cause of the water only trickling into the submarine when it should have gushed in at speed. The Inquiry decided that the failure to escape had nothing to do with faulty valves but was instead due to 'poor drill, ignorance and lack of leadership'.

No mention was made of the unsuccessful attempt which blocked the escape hatch.

Despite the compelling evidence heard to the contrary, the Inquiry decided that the crew was to blame for the entire tragedy. Their decision was based on the failure of the crew to close watertight doors, which the Inquiry called a failure to take 'adequate steps to prevent unrestricted flooding'. No matter that when the *Untamed* was examined it was noted that one watertight door was found to be inexplicably warped and incapable of being closed.

There was one question that those at the Inquiry could not satisfactorily answer and that is why the Ottway Log Tank should have been in use when the *Untamed* was carrying out a dive to periscope depth. It was accepted that this was a very unusual time to operate the device and it could only be suggested that it was being inspected at the time of the dive because it had a fault. Indeed it did and the valve stuck in the open position which meant that water poured into the *Untamed* through a 3-inch gap in the hull.

Within the space of a few short weeks, two separate Boards of Inquiry had come to the conclusion that the loss of a total of 74 men and two brand new submarines had been due to accident or negligence. Yet, until this time, not one submarine had been lost on its 'working up' trials.

But these findings did not correspond with the views held by certain individuals, some of whom occupied high positions in the Navy. One, Rear Admiral Claud Barry, was the top man in charge of the Navy's submarines. He began collecting what evidence there was available, not only relating to the *Vandal* and *Untamed*, but also citing two other vessels, HMS *Unswerving* and *Untiring*, both built by Vickers-Armstrong on Tyneside.

He referred to two incidents that happened to these vessels while under construction. *Unswerving* inexplicably toppled onto her side from her blocks, causing some damage, while the *Untiring* suffered an on-board explosion, which resulted in a small fire.

It was Barry who first raised the matter in a memo to the Admiralty. He declared that these losses and 'accidents' were suspicious. He suspected they may have been the result of sabotage in the yards and he wanted it to be investigated.

Although the links between these incidents were strong, he could have made his case even stronger if he had included another Barrow-built submarine, HMS *Usk*. *Usk* was launched in the middle of 1940, and after 'working up' trials in the Firth of Clyde, posted to the Mediterranean theatre of war for the start of 1941. The submarine only just made it to Malta using one engine. An abrasive compound was found in her failed engine and there was no way that it could have got there other than by someone deliberately inserting it. It was deemed an act of sabotage. For four months, the *Usk* was out of commission whilst being repaired. On her first patrol in May 1941, she was lost with all crew.

A few months after the tragic losses of both the *Vandal* and the *Untamed*, the next submarine out of Vickers at Barrow was HMS *Venturer*. Again, during trials in the Clyde, two serious faults were identified and remedied by the crew. Failure to pick up on these faults could have meant the submarine going the same way as either the *Vandal* or the *Untamed*.

All in all, here were six submarines built by Vickers-Armstrong yards—three from Tyneside and three from Barrow. Could it be that both yards had a saboteur, or saboteurs, among the workforce?

The fact that there were people employed in many of the war industries who held opposing views to those of the majority of their workmates and who hoped for a different outcome to the war has been well documented. Aircraft factories and munitions plants had their share of subversive employees. The shipyards were not immune from them either.

Another suggestion put forward was that the High Walker yard in Tyneside was unused to building submarines, its speciality being heavy warships. However, such was the Navy's continual need for all types of vessels that every shipyard in the country was working to full capacity, either repairing damaged vessels or building new ones to replace those lost, and had orders to fulfil for at least one submarine.

The frenzy of work in all shipbuilding yards in the country meant that almost every vessel was launched before its time. Faults occurred and were corrected on a daily basis. Yet, even so, are we to believe that out of six vessels built by Vickers-Armstrong, four had possibly potentially fatal flaws that manifested themselves by chance?

While there may be a case for the Tyneside yard citing the inexperience of the workforce as an excuse, it cannot be used in the case of the Barrow yard, who were dedicated submarine builders. It was this yard that the *Usk* came from, and out of the six vessels, her problem was irrefutably the result of sabotage.

There is one point that Barry may not have considered when drawing up his report to the Admiralty. If he were to ignore the shipyard 'accidents' to *Unswerving* and *Untiring*—falling off the building ways has happened to many a vessel, while the explosion on the *Untiring* was allegedly caused by some workers having a fly cigarette in a place where smoking was banned for obvious reasons—then the four other submarines have one fact in common. Each had visited the 3rd Submarine Flotilla base on the Clyde and their respective problems arose thereafter. Perhaps the saboteur worked there?

The idea is not that far-fetched when it is remembered that HMS *Usk*'s problems with her engines arose fully *six months* after her launch. She was in the Clyde when she received her orders to go to the Mediterranean.

The theories of Rear Admiral Barry were looked into, according to some reports on the orders of Prime Minister Winston Churchill himself. The results of the investigations have never been released and probably will not be in the foreseeable future, so it comes down to speculation.

The assumption is that HMS *Vandal* was lost due to a fatal fault. We still do not know what the fault was. For over 50 years, she remained missing, thought to be lying at the bottom of the deep Arran Trench. One man, businessman Sandy Young from Glasgow, had been collecting evidence for a great many years. He presented his wealth of material to the Royal Navy, who were able to confirm his suspicions and, using sonar, locate a wrecked submarine in 1994 lying in 300 feet of water just outside Lochranza Bay.

The Navy went further and videoed the wreck, which positively identified her as the *Vandal*. The video gives no clues as to any possible reason for the sinking. The area she now lies in is well outside the original search area from 1943. Tantalisingly, it is less than a quarter of a mile away from where the oil slick was reported by search aircraft.

With hindsight, it now looks like the crew could have been jettisoning oil in an effort to attract attention on the surface and, at the same time, trying to make the *Vandal* light enough to refloat. Or possibly the oil escaped from some damaged part of the craft, remained on the surface when the *Vandal* hit the bottom and by the time the slick was seen, about 14.10 hours in the following afternoon, the crew had already perished. No one can say what would have happened if this clue had been acted upon at the time.

The *Untamed* was salvaged and refitted and returned to duty with a new name. She became another member of the 'new' V-Class and was known as HMS *Vitality*. The superstitious among the Navy men would have been delighted to learn that she was to spend her time, not on active duty, but as a training vessel.

We know exactly what happened to each submarine, apart from the *Vandal*. Her wreck has, since being located, been officially classed as a war grave and therefore cannot be disturbed.

People like Sandy Young feel it is their duty to tell the complete story and they are pressing the authorities today for a fuller investigation. Others prefer to leave the past to the history books and suggest that nothing would be gained by the opening up of painful old sores. They are happy just to know now where their relatives lie and in order to mark the event, unveiled a memorial cairn to the crew of the *Vandal* in May 1997 on a hill just outside Lochranza overlooking the site of the tragic loss.

But will we ever know for certain if the *Vandal,* or any of the other five submarines, were victims of sabotage? In the interests of fairness, the possibility that no sabotage was involved in any of the events surrounding the six submarines must also be considered. It may simply be the case that other factors were to blame. Perhaps the tragedies could have been caused by design faults or by the use of inferior quality fittings. The constant strain on the shipyard workers to 'get it right every time' could have had a bearing on the incidents, in which case we are dealing with a series of accidents.

Or does the truth lie somewhere in the middle ground?

Ten
A FLIGHT TO OBLIVION

Mull is a delightful and peaceful island that sits off the west coast of Scotland. Blessed with rugged scenery, and, thanks to the Gulf Stream, a temperate climate, it is the haven of 2,500 residents and 10,000 deer. Strange then that this idyllic setting should keep the whole of the country mystified for ten years thanks to an incident that became known as 'the Great Mull Air Mystery'.

On Saturday 20th December 1975, Norman Peter Gibbs, a 55-year-old company director from London, along with a companion, Mrs Felicity Chadwick, or Grainger as she preferred to be known, a 32-year-old university lecturer, arrived on Mull aboard the car ferry from Oban. They booked into the Glen Forsa Hotel, near the village of Salen, on the island's east coast.

Gibbs was the managing director of Gibbs & Rae, which dealt in property development and through a subsidiary firm, Kelvinside Properties, owned properties in Glasgow. However, he had started the company only three years before, as he was also a talented musician who had previously, but at separate times, been the leader of both the BBC's Scottish Symphony Orchestra and the London Symphony Orchestra.

Gibbs was said to have been looking for a new challenge and that is why he came to be on Mull a few days before Christmas 1975. He was hoping to buy property and had expressed an interest in the luxury Western Isles Hotel in Tobermory. If this idea were to come to fruition, other properties owned by Gibbs's various companies would need to be sold in order to raise the necessary finance.

The day after his arrival, Gibbs found out that there was a single-engine aircraft available for hire at North Connel airport, about five miles outside Oban on the mainland. Gibbs telephoned the owner, Ian Hamilton, and made a verbal arrangement to hire the plane.

The name Ian Hamilton may possibly come to mind in relation to other matters, involving no little mystery in themselves. It was he who, along with others, was involved in the removal of the Stone of Destiny from Westminster Abbey in 1950.

Gibbs explained that he was not in possession of his pilot's licence or log book as he never considered the possibility that an aircraft would have been available. He suggested to Hamilton that he could check on his credentials by telephone. Hamilton did just that, phoning David Howitt, son of the owner of the Glen Forsa Hotel, who told him that he had seen Gibbs flying planes into the small airstrip which was next to the hotel. Satisfied, Hamilton agreed to deliver the aircraft to Glen Forsa the following day. Unfortunately, the following day was a cloudy one and Hamilton did not want to risk flying to Mull, so he telephoned Gibbs to tell him the news. Gibbs was disappointed but made arrangements for Hamilton to uplift him at Oban quay at 10 a.m. the next morning. Gibbs would come and collect the plane himself.

The weather was much better on Tuesday 23rd December. Hamilton met Gibbs as arranged, and, accompanied by Grainger, the three of them drove to North Connel. Once at the airport, Gibbs had his first sight of the red and white Cessna F150H aircraft, registration mark G-AVTN. It had been built by Reims Aviation in France in 1968, and bought by Hamilton four months previously in September 1975.

Hamilton set to work immediately, giving Gibbs the information on the aircraft and carrying out the pre-flight checks. By Gibbs's own admission, he was not too familiar with this particular model, having spent most of his recent flying time on twin-engine craft. However, he had flown Cessna planes many times before.

Hamilton was impressed with Gibbs's knowledge, especially in the safety check drill. Twice Hamilton missed out part of the check drill, but Gibbs did the check himself. The plane's engine was started and about 10 minutes later Gibbs and Grainger took off, heading in the general direction of Mull. The aircraft had a full tank of fuel, about 21.5 gallons, which gave it an average flying time of three and a half hours. Hamilton had also explained that North Connel was the only place in the surrounding area that Gibbs could re-fuel, if that were required.

So impressed was he, that later that day Hamilton telephoned

The missing Cessna aircraft G-AVTN. (D. Howitt)

Gibbs's hotel and left a message asking whether, when he returned the aircraft, he would he be prepared to spare some time and show Hamilton a few of his techniques.

The airstrip at Glen Forsa was a grass one about 900 yards long and 30 yards wide, constructed by a company of Royal Engineers on land owned by the Forestry Commission and leased to the then Argyll County Council. It had been in existence for about ten years.

The next day, Gibbs and Grainger took off from the airstrip in the Cessna about 8.30 a.m. and 55 minutes later landed at Broadford in Skye. Having spent all day on Skye, looking at property available for purchase, they arrived back on Mull about 4.10 p.m.

Both Gibbs and Grainger returned to their hotel and about 5.30 p.m. had a glass of whisky each before going on to have dinner in the hotel around 7.45. In addition to the food, each had a glass of red wine. After finishing his meal, Gibbs stated that it would be an ideal time to try out his theory that night landings at Glen Forsa were a distinct possibility, although the little airstrip had no runway lights.

Gibbs had said that he was trying to assess the viability of operating an air ambulance service, but it is more likely that in wanting to purchase a local hotel he was looking at the feasibility of guests arriving at all times and not being dictated to by the island's ferry timetable.

The previous evening, Gibbs had carried out a quick survey to see how visible the airstrip was in the dark. The lights of the hotel and some flashing navigational beacons in the nearby Sound of Mull gave him some hope that night landings were possible.

Gibbs spoke with Roger Howitt, manager of the hotel, and informed him of his intentions. Gibbs was in no mood to listen to any objections that anyone might want to raise, although none did. His mind was made up and he only told Howitt out of politeness.

Gibbs and Grainger went straight from the hotel to the aircraft about 9.15 p.m. They had borrowed two torches, which Gibbs intended using as makeshift runway lights. The plane's engine was started and warmed-up and then Gibbs taxied it to the furthest point of the airstrip at the eastern end.

Grainger got out of the aircraft here, and, on Gibbs's instructions, placed the two lit torches about a foot apart, facing the aircraft. Gibbs was taking off from this point and he would be coming in to land in this direction. He hoped he would be able to spot the torches from the air to aid his landing.

Meanwhile, back at the hotel, Roger Howitt, his wife and his sister-in-law had gone to an upstairs lounge, whose windows gave an uninterrupted view of the airstrip. Howitt's brother, David, who lived in a chalet within the grounds of the hotel with his wife, heard the sound of the Cessna's Rolls-Royce Continental engine being fired up and came out to see what was happening.

At this point, the first mysterious circumstance of the whole affair makes an appearance. At least two witnesses later stated that they had seen the moving torchlights but that the beams were too far apart to have been held by one person. Their impression was that there were two persons walking around both the plane and runway. Yet Grainger was to say later that only she had the torches on the runway as Gibbs remained in the aircraft throughout.

Was there another, third person out there on the runway? Could it be that what the witnesses saw was the beam of a torch reflected from the plane, which in parts was white in colour? However, these questions were never adequately answered because other, greater mysteries concerning this night arose.

The throttle of the aircraft was opened up and after about 200 yards, it became airborne. As the plane climbed into the dark night sky, all those watching could see the Cessna's lights, which were switched off momentarily, then on and finally off again, as Gibbs climbed to a height of around 500 feet, heading towards Salen.

Those on the ground watched as the plane turned slowly and then came towards them, flying down the Sound of Mull towards Craignure and the south of the island. Very soon, the plane disappeared out of sight due to a tree-line in the distance.

Grainger stood waiting patiently on the airstrip, expecting the plane to come back into view about 20 seconds later. Gibbs had told her that he would do the first 'circuit' solo, and, if successful, land and pick her up and then go and do some more with her on board. After a few minutes she was joined by David Howitt, and together they scanned the night skies and listened intently for any sign of the aircraft. There was none.

Grainger returned to the hotel about 10 p.m. in a distressed condition. Just prior to her arrival, some of the spectators thought they saw a light or flare out over the waters of the Sound of Mull. The light lasted only a short period, about 15 or 20 seconds, but no one was certain as to what it was.

Grainger was comforted by the suggestion of others that Gibbs, in all probability, had decided against a night landing on Mull and opted instead to head for either Glasgow or Prestwick or even Machrihanish on the Mull of Kintyre, all airstrips equipped to handle night traffic. Even so, Grainger, along with others, piled into cars and headed off for the grassy runway, illuminated it with the vehicles' headlights and began a search of the surrounding area, concentrating on the landing approach zone. They found nothing.

Just after 10.30 p.m. David Howitt contacted Air Traffic Control at Prestwick and gave them an account of what had taken place. It was not until 11.20 p.m., almost two hours after Gibbs took off, that the local police were advised of the situation.

The police, in the form of a sergeant from Tobermory and the village constable from Salen, arrived and took charge of the situation. They checked with Connel airport on the mainland but found that no planes had arrived that evening. With the limited resources available to them at this time, the two officers and David Howitt searched from Glen Forsa to Leiter Point, including Pennygown Hill, which was the only high obstacle in the direction that Gibbs was expected to take coming into land. They found nothing.

All the searching was carried out in horrendous weather conditions, with driving sleet and snow which had started about half an hour after Gibbs had taken off.

At first light on Christmas Day, the Glen Forsa Hotel became the nerve centre of a massive hunt for Gibbs and the plane. Police and RAF Kinloss Mountain Rescue Teams were flown to the island. Coastguards, Forestry Commission and Department of Agriculture workers and island volunteers were also involved and because of the size of area to be searched—basically the whole island—helicopters from both the RAF and Naval Air Sea Rescue were drafted in. Two of the helicopters were fitted with sonar equipment and they concentrated on scanning areas of the sea around Mull.

The hundreds of searchers on the ground were formed into lines, each man being within talking distance of the next, and in this way they combed the entire island. Unfortunately for them, the search was carried out in blizzard conditions. The snow, which had started falling on Christmas Eve continued to blanket the island without a break until well into Boxing Day.

The search continued day after day until, by Monday 29th December, the entire island and parts of the mainland across the Sound of Mull had been searched by the helicopters and by those on foot on the ground.

With the search having nowhere else to go, it was now at an end. By the following day, only a few local volunteers remained. No trace of either Gibbs or the Cessna had been found. It seemed that both had vanished off the face of the earth. The national press was full of theories, some sensible, most sensational, but then this was an ideal story for them.

As the speculation continued, the local police continued to search the shore area around the airstrip on an almost daily basis for all of January 1976, as they were certain that if the plane had crashed on land, the full scale search would have located it. During one of the searches a piece of aluminium with red paint on it was found on the shore by David Howitt, but when it was shown to Ian Hamilton he declared it to have nothing to do with his Cessna.

For four months the mystery continued until one morning in April, a local shepherd, Donald MacKinnon, came across a badly decomposed

The exact spot where the body of Peter Gibbs was found. The Sound of Mull can be seen in the distance. (D. Howitt)

body about 400 feet up on a hillside and about a mile from the runway. MacKinnon summoned the police, who in turn sent for David Howitt in order to identify the corpse as the police officers involved had never met Gibbs. Howitt was certain that it was Gibbs, remembering him from the clothes he had been wearing. The clothes on the body were the same, although the colours had faded considerably. Unfortunately, due to the level of decomposition and attacks on the body by birds and animals, there was no other way of positive identification at this time. Later, dental records confirmed it as Norman Peter Gibbs.

The body had been found lying on its back, the legs either side of a fallen tree trunk and the head touching the ground. Various suggestions have been made as to how the body came to be in this position. The idea given most credence was that Gibbs had been heading in a *downhill* direction.

The finding of the body threw up a number of questions, not least why it had not been found before now. The hill search squads had been on this particular hillside on at least two occasions but had not come across the body. Had the body been placed here after the hunt for Gibbs and his plane had ceased?

The new theory was that Gibbs had crashed the plane further up the hill and had been walking down to safety. The reason that the aircraft had not been found was that it had fallen into one of the small lochs in these hills. A new search was instigated, with divers searching the lochs, but they found nothing to suggest that this is what happened. The mystery continued.

A Fatal Accident Inquiry into Gibbs's death was held at Oban Sheriff Court on 24th June 1976. It lasted two days, and, incredibly, the Inquiry heard that a detailed post mortem revealed no injuries whatsoever on Gibbs's body, apart from a small cut on the left leg. The doctor who had carried out the examination of the corpse stated that its condition was in keeping with it having lain in the open for four months. This declaration negated the idea that the body had been placed there after the full-scale search had ended.

However, the most significant fact to be revealed at the Inquiry was that Gibbs's body and clothes showed no traces of saltwater. This matter was discussed in great detail and it was thought that with the body having lain on the hillside for the long months of a Scottish winter the snow and rains would have washed all traces of salt from the body and clothes. However, as one mystery appeared to be solved, another came to the fore again—where was the plane?

A number of expert witnesses who gave evidence discounted the numerous theories, including those of Gibbs having jumped from the plane while it was in flight, as he had no parachute and his body had no injuries. They also rejected claims that the reason the plane could not be found was that it had been totally burned up in a fierce fire or that it had fallen into the sea!

The findings of the Inquiry were that Gibbs had died of exposure and the proceedings were brought to a close with the words of the Procurator Fiscal, Graeme Pagan: 'This Inquiry has taken some mystery out, but it has not taken all of the mystery out of this case and until the plane is found, if it is ever found at all, then the mystery will remain.'

As if there was not enough mystery, in November 1976, four months after the end of the Inquiry, a local farmer on Mull, Robert Duncan, found an aircraft wheel covered in seaweed washed up on the shore at Kentallen, which is very close to Glen Forsa. Although it had no distinguishing marks on it, it was identified as a type of wheel fitted to Cessna planes.

For over ten long years, the mystery continued and was almost

Some of the headlines generated by the mysterious disappearance of Peter Gibbs and his aircraft. (D. Howitt)

forgotten about until on Wednesday 4th September 1986, when George Foster and brothers Richard and John Grieve, clam divers from Lochaline on the mainland, were diving in the Sound of Mull. About 100 feet down, they came across a red and white light aircraft lying on the seabed, minus its wings and engine. Both doors of the cockpit were jammed shut, but they did get to look inside and, to their relief, found it empty.

What the divers also noticed was that the plane was covered in seaweed and barnacles, but the word 'Cessna' was clearly visible, as was the aircraft's identifying mark, G-AVTN. There was no doubt that this was Gibbs's plane, but they did not realise the enormity of their find at the time and it was not until later that they notified the authorities.

One other discovery at the site disturbed the finders and that was the presence of a diver's flipper in the mud very close to the aircraft. Could it be that they were not the first people to discover Gibbs's' plane?

The aircraft was found to be lying about 500 yards from the shore of the island, with the windscreen and both door windows missing. The engine was discovered lying in the mud 10 yards in front of the plane and the wing was about 100 yards to the north of the aircraft's main body. One of the propeller blades was bent slightly backwards and the other appeared undamaged. One of the two wheels was found nearby, having broken off.

Now that the final piece of the jigsaw had been revealed, could it all be assembled to give some understanding of what had happened on Christmas Eve, 1975?

Again, the theories were expounded and claims and counter-claims made, but none really could resolve the matter. The problem in doing so seemed to lie in trying to explain why Gibbs's body was found so far away from the aircraft.

One of the most comprehensive investigations into the whole affair was carried out by the television programme '*Prosbaig*' (Telescope), broadcast shortly after Gibbs's plane had been found, which pulled all the facts together and gave answers to some of the questions that remained. The programme featured an expert, William Tench, who at this time was a Chief Advisor on Air Safety. At the time of Gibbs's disappearance in 1975, he was Chief Investigator of the Bureau of Air Investigations at Farnborough in England, a post he held for seven years.

Tench first of all examined the course Gibbs took that Christmas Eve. He was of the opinion that as Gibbs, at a height of about 100 feet, made his final turn over the Sound of Mull to come in for landing, he switched on the landing lights of the Cessna in an attempt to locate the surface of the sea. With the mist swirling at the height the aircraft was at, this is what possibly looked like a flare as seen by some onlookers that night.

The next point to be considered was the state of panic Gibbs must have been in when he could not get a sight of the airstrip. It was a matter of record that Gibbs had around 2,000 hours flying time throughout his life. 900 hours of this total was obtained during the Second World War, the majority of it being in training situations. In the 30-year period since then, he had accrued only a further 1100 hours, which meant that he was hardly flying on a regular basis.

Yet perhaps the most damning statement was that Gibbs only had a total of five hours experience of night flying, and that had all been obtained during the War! Tench stated that he had found similarities between Gibbs and himself in relation to War training and that when he checked back on his own Pilot's Log Book found that he himself had only six hours night flying experience during this time. A popular opinion expressed was that Gibbs was an experienced pilot. In reality, he was not.

Tench reckoned that pilot error had caused the engine to stop, explaining that the carburettor on Cessna 150's were, at low temperatures, prone to icing if not heated. With the weather of that night recorded as cold with sleet, Tench felt sure that this had occurred as the icing can happen at anything up to 10 degrees above freezing.

The former Chief Investigator then turned his investigative skills to the Cessna aircraft. Tench estimated that the plane dropped from 100 feet and hit the waters of the Sound of Mull at a speed of between 50 and 70 m.p.h. and at a shallow angle. The Cessna's engine had stopped prior to the impact, evidenced by only one of the propeller blades being bent. If the engine had been running, both blades would have been damaged.

The next, and probably most important question, was how Gibbs had come to be on the hillside. In the past, there has been a lot of speculation on this point. In his excellent book, *Scotland's Unsolved Mysteries of the Twentieth Century*, Richard Wilson writes that, after crashing his aircraft, Gibbs went up into the hillside in order to 'sit it out for a while', possibly for two reasons: that he was under the influence of alcohol and that his pilot's licence had expired.

In answer to the first claim, one glass of whisky and one of wine, over a four to five hour period does not suggest that Gibbs was intoxicated. What has perpetuated this myth is that the post mortem analysis showed Gibbs's body to have a high blood-alcohol count, greater than the limits for driving a car. This fact was dismissed as irrelevant by the authorities when it was explained that due to micro-organisms in the body, these levels can rise *after* death.

The matter of Gibbs's pilot's licence being revoked has long been the subject of debate. The truth of the matter is that he held a Private Pilot's Licence—no. 49508—which did not contain a rating allowing him to fly at night. The licence was also endorsed with the provision that the holder 'must wear spectacles to correct near/distant vision and to have another pair available whilst flying'. Yet no one had ever seen Gibbs wearing spectacles!

The confusion could have arisen due to Gibbs's brother stating previously that he (Gibbs) had had his licence suspended for medical reasons, possibly a heart complaint. However, records show that Gibbs had undergone a medical examination, which included a electro-cardiograph, six months before the accident. The tests showed no abnormality and he was passed fit to continue to fly. However, Gibbs did not take the compulsory flying test which was part of the licence renewal process, and this led to his licence lapsing.

What has been related in this chapter up to this point are the known facts which can be corroborated by witnesses, professional or other-wise, along with expert opinions based on experience.

What cannot be explained is why Gibbs's body was found an ex-traordinary distance from the crashed plane and with no serious in-jury. On these points the theorists and rumour-mongers have long speculated. The vast majority of theories as to how the body came to be there are more or less agreed on the following sequence of events.

Gibbs had no time to jump from the aircraft after it stalled and before it hit the water as he was flying a such a low altitude, but he managed to scramble clear and swim to the shore after the plane ditched. This involved swimming 500 yards in the right direction, fully clothed, on a cold and dark December night. But somehow he did it. Both the swim and the weather had taken its toll though, and when Gibbs got out of the water 20 or 25 minutes later, he was al-ready suffering greatly from hypothermia. He then stumbled from the shore and onto the main road.

At this point, if he had turned south and followed the road, it would have led him back to the hotel in about 10 minutes. Even better, if he had remained on the road, it is certain that he would have been spotted by any one of the number of cars whose occu-pants were taking part in the search for him. But Gibbs, in his to-tally confused and disorientated condition, continued blindly on across the road and up the hill, struggling over wet ground, two barbed wire fences—where he might have sustained the cut on his leg—and being constantly hammered by the driving sleet and snow.

As to the theory that Gibbs was coming down the hill, who can really say what was in his mind in the last few moments of his life? Perhaps, not surprisingly, he was walking, or more accurately, stumbling around in circles. Exhausted, he lay down, lapsed into unconsciousness and died.

One last feature of these theories was that Gibbs had planned his disappearance due to money worries. These rumours began after it was revealed that when he was a member of Glasgow Flying Club, based at the city's airport, he kept his own plane for a period of time. Gibbs failed to pay his bills for the maintenance of the aircraft and it was impounded until such time as he did pay. However, not long after this action, the plane was repossessed by a finance company which had provided Gibbs with a loan for the purchase of it. He had not paid them either. Yet his business accounts were found to be in first-class order when inspected after his death. His company was financially sound and his estranged wife inherited enough money to make her reasonably wealthy.

So much for the theories, which all rely on the assumption that Gibbs was the pilot, but the known facts of this strange case present a different picture and beg closer inspection. For some unexplained reason, Cessna G-AVTN has never been lifted from its final resting place on the sea-bed. Tench, of necessity, based his findings on film footage and stills of the aircraft *in situ*, taken by the programme makers. It also means that the plane has not been subjected to a close examination by Air Accident Investigators, who would quickly be able to decide, once and for all, if the impact damage to the aircraft would have been a survivable experience for the pilot. From the information available at present, it would seem that this was not the case.

The wings of the Cessna aircraft had been torn off and now lay 100 yards away from the main body on the sea-bed. The engine had been wrenched from its mountings and rested 10 yards in front of the fuselage. The windscreen and both door windows were missing, presumed smashed. Both doors were locked when it was found and, at first, the instrument panel was thought to be missing, but it too had been violently shifted from its position and was later found to have fallen further down into the cockpit.

The accumulation of damage to the plane suggests an abrupt and violent end to the Cessna's short flight, a sort of nose dive into the sea and oblivion. Yet, if this is what happened, then how was it that Gibbs was not injured?

The conclusion that then has to be drawn from this is that Gibbs was not in the plane when it crashed into the Sound of Mull. Yet, if we are to believe the evidence put forward to the Inquiry by Board of Trade Accident Investigator, William Cairns—and there is no reason to doubt it—that it would be impossible for Gibbs to jump from the aircraft while in flight. It must also be remembered that he had no parachute, no injuries as such and both doors were locked. All this leads to a final conclusion: someone else was flying the aircraft!

This idea is not that far-fetched when it is recalled that evidence from two or more witnesses at the hotel say that they saw two torchlights moving simultaneously but, judging from their beams, they were too far apart to have been held by one person. They all thought that there were three people around the revving-up plane.

With Gibbs not in the aircraft and it having failed to return to the airstrip as scheduled, did he, like the others later searching for the plane, climb the nearest hill to gain a vantage point to look out for the overdue Cessna? Or, seeing the torchlights of the searching police officers and David Howitt coming in his direction, make off up the hill in front of them in an effort to avoid discovery? Before he felt it safe to return, the severe winter weather could have exacted a heavy toll.

Even at this late stage, it is possible that the mystery could still be solved beyond any doubt. It would not be a costly exercise to raise the wreckage of G-AVTN today and subject it to close inspection. Quite a bit of the plane will never be found, thanks to over ten years of weekend pleasure divers taking pieces of it as souvenirs, but any accident damage will still be clearly visible. If the aircraft was to be recovered, a cursory search of the surrounding sea-bed should also be carried out at the same time. Perhaps all that would reveal are the bones of a skeleton belonging to a long dead pilot. Then the new question to be asked would be: who was the mystery flier?

Until such time as the aircraft is raised the eye-witness statements must carry the most weight and they say that Gibbs was flying the plane. If they are to be believed, then it could be that the mystery surrounding these tragic events only sprang up because of one man's determined efforts to survive at all costs.

SOURCES CONSULTED

Books

Amstrong, Warren *White for Danger: True Dramas of Lightships and Lighthouses* (London, 1963)

Begg, Fido and Skinner *The A - Z of Jack The Ripper* (London, 1996)

Cassells, Ian, *No More Paraffin Oilers* (Caithness, 1994)

Everitt, Don, *The K-Boats* (London, 1963)

House, Jack, *Murder not Proven* (Glasgow, 1984)

Lazarus, Richard *Beyond the Impossible: a Twentieth Century Almanac of the Unexplained* (London, 1994)

Macadam, Scott, *The Great Mull Air Mystery* (Isle of Mull, 1986)

MacGregor, Alasdair Alpin, *The Farthest Hebrides* (London, 1969)

Moore, John W, *Notable Scottish Trials: The Trial of A. J. Monson* (Glasgow, 1908)

Nesbit, Roy, 'What Did Happen To The Duke Of Kent?' in *Aeroplane Monthly*, January and February 1990

Nicholson, Christopher, *Rock Lighthouses of Britain* (Cambridge, 1983)

Owen, Neil and Jones, Phil, *Airfield Focus* (Oban, 1997)

Roughead, William, *Notable Scottish Trials: The Trial of Dr Pritchard* (Glasgow, 1906)

Wilson, Richard, *Scotland's Unsolved Mysteries of the Twentieth Century* (London, 1989)

Wolf, A. P., *Jack the Myth* (London, 1993)

Newspapers

Daily Record
The Herald
The Scotsman

INDEX